Intercultural Competence and Pragmatics

Gila A. Schauer

Intercultural Competence and Pragmatics

palgrave
macmillan

Gila A. Schauer
Sprachwissenschaft
University of Erfurt
Erfurt, Thüringen, Germany

ISBN 978-3-031-44471-5   ISBN 978-3-031-44472-2 (eBook)
https://doi.org/10.1007/978-3-031-44472-2

© The Author(s) 2024. This is an Open access publication.
Open Access This book is licensed under the terms of the Creative Commons Attribution 4.0 International License (http://creativecommons.org/licenses/by/4.0/), which permits use, sharing, adaptation, distribution and reproduction in any medium or format, as long as you give appropriate credit to the original author(s) and the source, provide a link to the Creative Commons licence and indicate if changes were made.
The images or other third party material in this book are included in the book's Creative Commons licence, unless indicated otherwise in a credit line to the material. If material is not included in the book's Creative Commons licence and your intended use is not permitted by statutory regulation or exceeds the permitted use, you will need to obtain permission directly from the copyright holder.
The use of general descriptive names, registered names, trademarks, service marks, etc. in this publication does not imply, even in the absence of a specific statement, that such names are exempt from the relevant protective laws and regulations and therefore free for general use.
The publisher, the authors, and the editors are safe to assume that the advice and information in this book are believed to be true and accurate at the date of publication. Neither the publisher nor the authors or the editors give a warranty, expressed or implied, with respect to the material contained herein or for any errors or omissions that may have been made. The publisher remains neutral with regard to jurisdictional claims in published maps and institutional affiliations.

Cover pattern © Melisa Hasan

This Palgrave Macmillan imprint is published by the registered company Springer Nature Switzerland AG.
The registered company address is: Gewerbestrasse 11, 6330 Cham, Switzerland

Paper in this product is recyclable.

In memory of and dedicated to
Zoltán Dörnyei

Copyright Acknowledgements

I am grateful to the following publishers for granting permission to reproduce the following figures:

- Figure 2.1, Byram's (2021) model of intercultural competence and intercultural communicative competence, reprinted from *Teaching and assessing intercultural communicative competence*, 2nd edition, Michael Byram, page 84, 2021, with permission from Multilingual Matters.
- Figure 2.2, Fantini's (1995) conceptualization of the link between world views and language, reprinted from *International Journal of Intercultural Relations*, 19/2, Alvino E. Fantini, Introduction—Language, culture and world view: Exploring the nexus, page 151, 1995, with permission from Elsevier.

Acknowledgements

I would like to begin this book by paying tribute to my late supervisor Zoltán Dörnyei, who passed away in 2022. This book would not exist without him.

When I first went to Nottingham in 2000 to study for my MA in English Studies, I started my postgraduate degree with the vague idea that I loved English and that I wanted to learn more about it. At the end of my master's studies, having attended all of Zoltán's seminars and having been so fortunate to have him as my MA dissertation supervisor, I knew that I wanted to focus on pragmatics and do my PhD on interlanguage pragmatic development with him. Zoltán was a wonderful teacher—enthusiastic, engaging and kind. He was able to bring the topics he taught to life by sharing personal anecdotes and by encouraging us to really reflect on a wide variety of issues relevant to foreign and second language learning and teaching that we could subsequently explore in research assignments. Through him I encountered many of the concepts addressed in this book: communicative competence, pragmatics, intercultural (communicative) competence. He made me see how my interests in linguistics could come together and was instrumental in shaping my career as a researcher and educator. I will forever be grateful to him for everything he taught me.

With Zoltán's gentle guidance I took my first steps as a researcher. While at Nottingham, then at Lancaster and later at Erfurt, I had many conversations about intercultural communication and pragmatics that influenced my thoughts on the issues addressed in this book. Thank you for sharing your thoughts with me to (in approximate chronological order) Rebecca Hughes (thank you also for allowing me to include a discussion from your seminar), Ben Woolhead, Tomoko Ishii, Khawla Zahran, Mike Handford, Sung Il-Lee, Nicole Detzer, Ingrid Tessmer, Laura Bond, the late Alan Waters, the late Geoffrey Leech, Martin Bygate, Jayanti Banerjee, Michal Krzyzanowski, Jane Sunderland, Nicola Halenko, Chia-Chun Lai, Sadegh Sadeghidizaj, Masoud Shaghaghi, Naoko Osuka, Annick De Houwer, Beate Hampe, Susanne Hoppe, Csaba Földes, Theresia Piszczan, Verena Laschinger, Matthias Altmann, Sandra Schmidt, Susanne Knapp, Maria Economidou-Kogetsidis, Fikry Boutros, Milica Savić, Anders Myrset, Stefan Maier, Karen Glaser and Sandie Mourão.

I am also grateful to the pre-sessional English for Academic Purposes (EAP) teachers at Lancaster University and the teachers at the language centre of the University of Erfurt—thank you for all our discussions.

I would also like to express my gratitude to my former and current students at the universities of Nottingham, Lancaster and Erfurt. Thank you for sharing your thoughts, views and experiences of intercultural interactions with me.

Thank you also to all colleagues who forwarded the invitation to take part in this research and thereby made it happen.

I am also very much indebted to the participants of this study. Thank you for taking the time to complete the survey and share your views and perspectives with me.

I am grateful to the members of Cultnet: Intercultural Community for Researchers and Educators, an international research group interested in language, culture and education, for their warm welcome and interesting discussions on the mailing list. I would particularly like to thank Natalia Morollón Martí and Ulla Margareta Lundgren for sharing materials, checking translations and answering questions on Scandinavian languages and Spanish as a foreign language.

This publication was supported by Open Access Funds of the State of Thuringia and by the University of Erfurt for which I am very grateful.

Many thanks also to Cathy Scott and Arunaa Devi at Palgrave for advice, guidance and support, to Tim Curnow for copyediting the manuscript and to the anonymous reviewers for their insightful comments.

I am also grateful to Troy McConachy, who with Anthony Liddicoat, co-edited a recent volume on pragmatics and intercultural understanding and whose editorial comments inspired me to explore the issues addressed in this book.

Growing up in a context in which different languages and different varieties were spoken showed me the fascinating aspects and the potential of multilingual environments and multilingualism. I am grateful to my grandparents, aunts, uncles and cousins, as well as Marc Van Noten, Zaida Baumgärtner and Astrid Hübschmann for letting me encounter different ways of communicating.

My deepest gratitude goes to my parents—thank you for your love, wisdom and great sense of humour.

Contents

1 Introduction 1
   References 4

2 Background 7
   2.1 Pragmatics and Pragmatic Competence 7
   2.2 Culture 15
   2.3 Communicative Competence 19
   2.4 Intercultural (Communicative) Competence 22
   References 30

3 Methodology 39
   3.1 Participants 39
   3.2 Instrument 44
   3.3 Procedure 45
   Appendix: Survey Questions 45
   References 51

4 Results: Components of Intercultural Competence 53
   4.1 Overview of Terms Associated with Intercultural
       Competence in the L2 53
   4.2 Linguistic Components of Intercultural Competence 61
   4.3 Summary 66
   References 67

5 Results: Aspects of Modern Foreign Language Teaching in Higher Education — 71
5.1 Importance of Academic and General Skills and Competences — 71
5.2 Importance of Teaching Language Aspects — 74
5.3 Importance of Teaching Information Pertaining to L2 Countries and Cultures — 80
5.4 Importance of Materials and Texts Covering Specific Topics — 85
5.5 Summary — 90
References — 92

6 Results: The Relationship Between Intercultural and Pragmatic Competence — 95
6.1 Teachers' Familiarity with Pragmatic Competence — 95
6.2 Teachers' Views on the Relationship Between Intercultural and Pragmatic Competence — 98
6.3 Summary — 101
References — 102

7 Results: Intercultural Competence and Gender-Neutral Language — 105
7.1 Teachers' Views on the Existence of Gender-Neutral Language Options — 105
7.2 Teaching Gender-Neutral Language Options or Not — 110
7.3 Summary — 115
References — 122

8 Results: Intercultural Competence in Modern Foreign Language Teacher Education — 125
8.1 Coverage of Intercultural Competence in Higher Education — 125
8.2 Scholars Associated with Intercultural Competence — 129
8.3 Summary — 132
References — 133

9 Conclusion — 135
9.1 Summary of Findings — 135
  9.1.1 Chapter 4: Components of Intercultural Competence — 135
  9.1.2 Chapter 5: Aspects of L2 Teaching in Higher Education — 136

9.1.3	Chapter 6: The Relationship Between Intercultural and Pragmatic Competence	138
9.1.4	Chapter 7: Intercultural Competence and Gender-Neutral Language	139
9.1.5	Chapter 8: Intercultural Competence in Modern Foreign Language Teacher Education	139
9.2	Limitations	140
9.3	Implications	141
9.3.1	Theoretical Implications	141
9.3.2	Methodological Implications	145
9.3.3	Pedagogical Implications	146
References		147

Index 149

ABOUT THE AUTHOR

Gila A. Schauer is Professor of English and Applied Linguistics at the University of Erfurt, Germany. She received her MA and PhD from the University of Nottingham, UK. She is the author of two monographs—*Interlanguage Pragmatics Development: The Study Abroad Context* published by Continuum/Bloomsbury in 2009, and *Teaching and Learning English in the Primary School: Interlanguage Pragmatics in the EFL Context* published by Springer in 2019—as well as of several journal articles and chapters in edited volumes and handbooks. She was the Director of the EAP/Study Skills Programme at Lancaster University from 2005 to 2010 and Director of the Language Centre at the University of Erfurt from 2012 to 2014.

ABBREVIATIONS

CoE	Council of Europe
CLT	Communicative language teaching
CCSARP	Cross-Cultural Speech Act Realization Project
EAP	English for Academic Purposes
EFL	English as a foreign language
IC	Intercultural competence
ICC	Intercultural (communicative) competence
ILP	Interlanguage pragmatics
ISLA	Instructed second language acquisition
KMK	Kultusministerkonferenz [The Standing Conference of the Ministers of Education and Cultural Affairs of the Länder in the Federal Republic of Germany]
L1	First language, native language or mother tongue
L2	Second or foreign language
LGBTIQ	Lesbian, Gay, Bisexual, Trans, Intersex, Queer/Questioning
MFL	Modern foreign languages
SLA	Second language acquisition
TL	Target language
UNESCO	United Nations Educational, Scientific and Cultural Organization

List of Figures

Fig. 2.1	Byram's (2021) model of intercultural competence and intercultural communicative competence	25
Fig. 2.2	Fantini's (1995) conceptualization of the link between world view and language	28
Fig. 3.1	Age groups represented in the sample	40
Fig. 3.2	Years of teaching experience of the participants	41
Fig. 3.3	Course types taught by the respondents	43
Fig. 4.1	Percentage of teachers who marked each potential component as being associated with L2 intercultural competence	55
Fig. 4.2	Percentage of teachers who responded *yes*, *no* and *don't know* to whether each linguistic aspect is part of intercultural competence	63
Fig. 5.1	Percentage of teachers who responded that the teaching of each skill or competence in the L2 was very important or important	73
Fig. 5.2	Percentage of teachers who responded that the teaching of each language aspect in the L2 was very important or important	77
Fig. 5.3	Percentage of teachers who responded that the teaching of facts relating to L2 countries and cultures was very important or important	82
Fig. 5.4	Percentage of teachers who responded that materials and texts covering each specific topic was very important or important	87
Fig. 6.1	Teachers' familiarity with pragmatic competence (as a percentage of all teachers who responded)	96
Fig. 6.2	Teachers' views on the relationship between intercultural competence and pragmatic competence (as a percentage of all teachers)	99

Fig. 7.1	Existence of gender-neutral language options in the L2s they taught, according to the teachers (as a percentage of all teachers who responded)	106
Fig. 7.2	Teaching of gender-neutral language options by the participants (as a percentage of all teachers who responded)	110
Fig. 8.1	Coverage of intercultural competence in their higher education studies according to the participants (as a percentage of total responses)	126
Fig. 8.2	Coverage of intercultural competence in their higher education according to the participants, by age group	128
Fig. 8.3	Scholars whom participants associated with IC, ordered by the number of teachers who mentioned them	130
Fig. 9.1	Three-tier model of intercultural competence (based on teachers' ratings)	142
Fig. 9.2	Intercultural competence model	144

LIST OF TABLES

Table 3.1	Overview of the groups of teachers who taught each of the languages represented by more than three teachers	44
Table 4.1	Percentage of teachers in each language group who selected each potential component as being associated with intercultural competence	56
Table 4.2	Percentage of teachers in each language group who selected each potential linguistic aspect as being part of intercultural competence	65
Table 5.1	Teachers' evaluations of the importance of teaching selected skills and competences in the L2	72
Table 5.2	Teachers' evaluations of the importance of teaching language aspects	75
Table 5.3	Averages of teachers' evaluations of the importance of teaching individual language aspects, for each language group	79
Table 5.4	Teachers' evaluations of the importance of teaching facts and information about L2 countries and cultures	81
Table 5.5	Averages of teachers' evaluations of the importance of teaching facts and information about the L2 countries and cultures, for each language group	84
Table 5.6	Teachers' evaluations of the importance of materials and texts covering specific topics	86
Table 5.7	Averages of teachers' evaluations of the importance of materials and texts covering specific topics, for each language group	89
Table 6.1	Teachers' familiarity with pragmatic competence according to language group	96

Table 6.2	Teachers' views on the relationship between intercultural competence and pragmatic competence, for each language group	100
Table 7.1	Existence of gender-neutral language options, according to the teachers of each specific language	107
Table 7.2	Teaching of gender-neutral language options by the participants in each language group who agreed that there were gender-neutral forms	111
Table 7.3	Teachers' reasons for teaching gender-neutral language (by language taught)	116
Table 7.4	Teachers' reasons for *not* teaching gender-neutral language (by language taught)	121
Table 8.1	Coverage of intercultural competence in their higher education according to the participants, for each age group	127
Table 8.2	Coverage of intercultural competence in their higher education according to the participants, for each language group	129
Table 8.3	Scholars whom participants in each language group associated with intercultural competence	131

CHAPTER 1

Introduction

While international organizations such as the United Nations Educational, Scientific and Cultural Organization (UNESCO, 2013) or the Council of Europe (CoE, 2014) agree that intercultural competence (IC) should play a key role in education, it is not always clear what IC may encompass in specific teaching contexts and subject areas. Researchers working in the field of second language (L2)[1] pragmatics would argue that pragmatics is at the core of intercultural competence, since linguistic pragmatics studies what constitutes (in)appropriate and (im)polite language use in different contexts and cultures.

However, when looking at the existing literature on intercultural competence, the link between IC and pragmatics is frequently not explicitly addressed, although it may be implicitly presumed (see Schauer, 2022). Notable exceptions are, for example, McConachy and Liddicoat (2016, p. 16) who "view meta-pragmatic awareness as a central feature of intercultural competence", Jackson (2019, p. 487), who writes that "L2 pragmatic competence and intercultural competence are closely related", and Taguchi and Roever (2017, p. 261), who argue that "pragmatic competence in intercultural settings can be viewed as a constituent of intercultural competence". The latter also make the very important point that "we

---

[1] The term *second language* or *L2* is used here to mean any language that is not the (or one of) learner's native language(s); see the footnote in Chap. 2 for details.

need more studies that examine the relationship between pragmatic competence and intercultural competence" (2017, p. 261).

This book answers the call for more research on the link between intercultural competence and pragmatics. It presents the results of a research project that explored the views of modern foreign language (MFL) teachers in higher education. Learning more about how MFL teachers in higher education conceptualize intercultural competence and the value they attach to, as well as the attention they give to, various areas of pragmatics in their teaching is very important, since those language professionals may be the final language teachers that learners encounter during their formal foreign language education. They are, therefore, in a unique position in shaping foreign language learners' intercultural and pragmatic awareness, competence and skills.

Data for the study were collected with an online survey that contained 18 items and sub-items (see Appendix in Chap. 3) and was available for participation from May to August 2021. The survey was completed by 133 teachers teaching a total of 15 different modern foreign languages. In addition to presenting the results of the complete group of 133 teachers, I will also frequently refer to subgroups of teachers when this seems relevant. In most cases this will involve a contrastive analysis of the six modern foreign languages that were focused on by three of more teachers in the survey: English, German, Italian, Spanish, French, Dutch and Swedish (presented according to group size).

The survey featured the following research questions; several of these contained a list of items to be ranked or evaluated (see the Appendix in Chap. 3)[2]:

1. How important is it for modern foreign language teachers in higher education to teach different skills and competences? [Followed by a list of nine items]
2. Which terms do the MFL teachers associate with intercultural competence in the language(s) they are teaching? [Followed by a list of 24 items]
3. Which linguistic aspects do the MFL teachers consider to be part of intercultural competence? [Followed by a list of 12 items]
4. How important is it for the MFL teachers to teach specific facts/information about the countries and cultures in which the language(s) they

---

[2] In addition to the research questions, the survey also featured questions about the teachers' personal backgrounds; see Appendix in Chap. 3.

are teaching is/are (an) official language(s) or native language(s)? [Followed by a list of 16 items]
5. How important is it for the MFL teachers to include texts and materials focusing on different issues and addressing experiences of individuals representing different groups in their language classes? [Followed by a list of 11 items]
6. How important is it for the MFL teachers to teach different aspects of the MFL? [Followed by a list of 19 items]
7a. Are the MFL teachers familiar with pragmatic competence?
7b. Do the MFL teachers consider pragmatic competence and intercultural competence to be connected?
8a. Do gender-neutral expressions or pronouns exist in the languages the MFL teachers are teaching? [Teachers who answered "yes" to question 8a proceeded on to questions 8b to 8d, the other teachers proceeded on to question 9]
8b. If gender-neutral language options exist in the languages the MFL teachers are teaching, do they teach them?
8c. If the MFL teachers are teaching gender-neutral language options, what are their reasons for doing so?
8d. If the MFL teachers are not teaching gender-neutral forms, what are their reasons for not doing so?
9a. Was intercultural competence addressed during the MFLs teachers' own university studies?
9b. Do the MFL teachers associate particular scholars with intercultural competence?

The results of the survey are presented in Chaps. 4 to 8. Chapter 4 focuses on what teachers consider to be the components of intercultural competence (questions 2 and 3). Chapter 5 addresses aspects of MFL teaching in higher education (questions 1, 4, 5 and 6). Chapter 6 explores teachers' views on the relationship between intercultural and pragmatic competence (questions 7a and 7b). Chapter 7 focuses on gender-neutral language (questions 8a–8d), while Chap. 8 addresses teachers' encounters with IC during their own studies and their awareness of scholars working in the field (questions 9a and 9b).

Depending on the individual reader's background and interests, they may wish to read the monograph not from beginning to end, but instead to focus on the issues that address their main interests. However, for readers mostly or entirely unfamiliar with pragmatics and intercultural competence, I would recommend reading the monograph chapter by chapter, in order. As the book is part of the Palgrave Pivot series, the review of the literature presented in the background chapter (Chap. 2) is concise and very much focused on the link between intercultural competence and pragmatics.[3] The methodology chapter (Chap. 3) provides information on the language teachers and also contains the full questionnaire in its Appendix. The conclusion chapter (Chap. 9) provides a summary of the findings of the research project and addresses the limitations of the study. It also features theoretical, methodological and pedagogical implications and presents two models of intercultural competence that are based on the results of the present project.

With the overall topic and the structure of this book now introduced, the next chapter lays the foundations for the study by providing an overview of pragmatics, culture, communicative competence and intercultural competence.

References

Council of Europe. (2014). *Developing intercultural competence through education*. Council of Europe Publishing.
Deardorff, D. K. (Ed.). (2009). *The SAGE handbook of intercultural competence*. Sage.
Jackson, J. (2019). Intercultural competence and L2 pragmatics. In N. Taguchi (Ed.), *The Routledge handbook of second language acquisition and pragmatics* (pp. 479–494). Routledge.
McConachy, T., & Liddicoat, A. J. (2016). Meta-pragmatic awareness and intercultural competence: The role of reflection and interpretation in intercultural mediation. In F. Dervin & Z. Gross (Eds.), *Intercultural competence in education: Alternative approaches for different times* (pp. 13–30). Palgrave.
Schauer, G. A. (2022). Intercultural competence and pragmatics in the L2 classroom: Views of in-service EFL teachers in primary, secondary and adult education. In T. McConachy & A. J. Liddicoat (Eds.), *Teaching and learning second language pragmatics for intercultural understanding* (pp. 173–191). Routledge.
Taguchi, N., & Roever, C. (2017). *Second language pragmatics*. Oxford University Press.
UNESCO. (2013). *Intercultural competences: Conceptual and operational framework*. UNESCO. https://unesdoc.unesco.org/ark:/48223/pf0000219768

---

[3] Readers interested in a much more comprehensive overview of intercultural competence models from a broad range of different perspectives and disciplines will find *The SAGE handbook of intercultural competence* edited by Deardorff (2009) a good source.

Open Access This chapter is licensed under the terms of the Creative Commons Attribution 4.0 International License (http://creativecommons.org/licenses/by/4.0/), which permits use, sharing, adaptation, distribution and reproduction in any medium or format, as long as you give appropriate credit to the original author(s) and the source, provide a link to the Creative Commons licence and indicate if changes were made.

The images or other third party material in this chapter are included in the chapter's Creative Commons licence, unless indicated otherwise in a credit line to the material. If material is not included in the chapter's Creative Commons licence and your intended use is not permitted by statutory regulation or exceeds the permitted use, you will need to obtain permission directly from the copyright holder.

CHAPTER 2

Background

2.1 PRAGMATICS AND PRAGMATIC COMPETENCE

Since pragmatics became part of the discipline of linguistics in the 1970s (Jucker, 2012),[1] numerous definitions of it have been put forward that highlight its different aspects and are sometimes broader or narrower (see, e.g., Barron et al., 2017; Culpeper & Schauer, 2018). One rather narrow but well-known definition is the one by Bardovi-Harlig (2013, p. 68) who defines "pragmatics [as] the study of how-to-say-what-to-whom-when"; this definition "highlights the speaker and use (how to say), the content (what), the hearer (who), and the context (when)" (Aslan, 2021, p. 173). While this definition could be considered to contain the core components of pragmatics, Bardovi-Harlig (2013, p. 69) herself notes that this is her "'cocktail party' definition, and although it is fairly accurate in spirit, it is lacking in the detail required for academic work".

To obtain a more detailed picture of what pragmatics focuses on, the following box presents perspectives on pragmatics that share common features but that also each highlight specific aspects of it.

---

[1] Linguistic pragmatics originated from the discipline of philosophy and certain developments in the field of linguistics in the mid-twentieth century (see, e.g., Jucker, 2012, for a historical overview).

> **Pragmatics**
> "Traditional language analysis contrasts pragmatics with syntax and semantics. [...] Whereas formal analyses of syntax and semantics do not consider the users of the linguistic forms that they describe and analyse, pragmatics deals very explicitly with the study of relationships holding between linguistic forms and the human beings who use these forms. As such, pragmatics is concerned with people's intentions, assumptions, beliefs, goals and the kinds of actions they perform while using language. Pragmatics is also concerned with contexts, situations, and settings within which such language uses occur". (Celce-Murcia & Olshtain, 2000, p. 19)
>
> "Pragmatics refers to the appropriate use of language in social interaction, along with the rules that govern interaction with others. Pragmatic language rules are defined as the effective and appropriate use of language to accomplish social goals, manage turns and topics in conversation, and express appropriate degrees of politeness, awareness of social roles and recognition of others' conversational needs (American Speech-Language-Hearing Association)". (Levey, 2017, p. 19)
>
> "Pragmatics is broadly defined as the study of language use in context from the perspective of speakers (users) and the effects language has on emotions and attitudes of interlocutors". (Félix-Brasdefer & Shively, 2021, p. 1)

The first definition, by Celce-Murcia and Olshtain (2000), positions pragmatics next to the related fields of syntax and semantics, thereby contrasting it with the subdisciplines of linguistics that focus on the grammatical structures of sentences and on word meaning, respectively. It also emphasizes the central role of language users and their wishes and communicative aims in pragmatics. Another important point made in the first definition is the significance of contextual factors in pragmatics, something which is also addressed in the third definition.

The second definition, that of Levey (2017), links pragmatics with *appropriate* and *effective* language use. As will be demonstrated in more detail in Sect. 2.4, this connects pragmatics with intercultural competence.

Like the first definition, this second one also addresses language users' goals in communication and firmly places linguistic politeness within pragmatics.

The third definition, by Félix-Brasdefer and Shively (2021), emphasizes that pragmatics does not solely focus on the speaker/writer but gives equal consideration to the hearer/reader and how they perceive language. This definition also echoes aspects of the well-known definition of pragmatics by Crystal (1985) regarding the effects of language use,[2] but refines it by explicitly referring to the effects on "emotions and attitudes" (Félix-Brasdefer & Shively, 2021, p. 1).

Based on the definitions of pragmatics presented above, pragmatics is concerned with the intentions and aims of language users and their use of language in an individual context, which should ideally be appropriate and effective and thus have the desired impact on their interlocutor and achieve their intended aim(s).

Pragmatics itself has several subdisciplines that are of relevance for the present study, in particular *cross-cultural pragmatics, interlanguage pragmatics*—now frequently also referred to as *second language pragmatics* or *L2 pragmatics*—and *variational pragmatics*.

> **Cross-Cultural Pragmatics**
> According to House and Kádár (2021, p. 1), "cross-cultural pragmatics encompasses the comparative study of the use of language by human beings in different languages and cultures", while Taguchi and Roever (2017, p. 3) note that "the main premise of cross-cultural pragmatics is that language use reflects the underlying values, beliefs and assumptions shared by members of the given speech community".

A very well-known example of cross-cultural pragmatic research is the Cross-Cultural Speech Act Realization Project, also frequently referred to as CCSARP, which was published in 1989 as a book edited by Shoshana Blum-Kulka, Juliane House and Gabriele Kasper. This international study

---

[2] In his definition, Crystal (1985, p. 240) refers to "effects their [speakers'] use of language has on other participants in the act of communication".

examined how requests and apologies were performed by speakers of a variety of languages, for example, English, French, German, Hebrew and Spanish. The project paved the way for further studies that would investigate differences and similarities across different languages and thus provide insights that may be helpful for MFL language learners and teachers (e.g., Bataineh & Bataineh, 2008; Chen et al., 2011; Culpeper et al., 2010; Schauer, 2017; Suszczyriska, 1999). While cross-cultural pragmatics contrasts the linguistic choices and the perceptions of native speakers of particular languages and cultures, interlanguage pragmatics focuses on learners of second or foreign languages.[3]

> **Interlanguage Pragmatics (ILP)**
> "Researchers working in interlanguage pragmatics are interested in a variety of issues that relate to L2 learners and their ability to (a) produce utterances that are appropriate and effective and therefore achieve their communicative aims, (b) understand L2 utterances that they encounter correctly. While some researchers tend to focus on how instruction (e.g., the use of particular teaching materials or instructional approaches) can help L2 learners produce appropriate language and enable them to correctly decode language directed at them, others are interested in how L2 learners' pragmatic skills develop outside of formal instructional contexts". (Schauer, 2019, p. 14)

As already mentioned above, in recent years, the terms *second language pragmatics* or *L2 pragmatics* have been used to describe the area of pragmatics that focuses on second or foreign language learners (e.g., Bardovi-Harlig, 2013; Culpeper et al., 2018; Roever, 2022). The term *interlanguage* was developed by Selinker in 1972 who used it

> to refer to the language produced by learners, both as a system which can be described at any one point in time as resulting from systematic rules, and as the series of interlocking systems that characterize learner progression. In other words, the interlanguage concept relies on two fundamental notions:

---

[3] The term *second language* refers to an additional language, that is, a language that is learned after the first language or the first languages (in case of multilingual children) that is learned in a country in which that language is the official language (e.g., learning French in France). In contrast, the term *foreign language* refers to an additional language that is learned in a country in which that language is not the official language (e.g., learning French in Poland).

the language produced by the learner is a system in its own right, obeying its own rules, and it is a dynamic system, evolving over time. (Mitchell et al., 2013, p. 36)

While the terms *L2 pragmatics* and *second language pragmatics* very overtly connect this subdiscipline of pragmatics to second language acquisition,[4] *interlanguage pragmatics* emphasizes the dynamic nature of the L2 system, as well as the notion that there is an underlying system, for example, that learners tend to go through various stages in their L2 pragmatic development, such as using less complex and more direct requests in the early stages of L2 learning and over time producing more complex and indirect requests in their L2. Both of the aforementioned aspects have been addressed in developmental studies in pragmatics (see, e.g., Achiba, 2003; Barron, 2003; Félix-Brasdefer, 2007; Glaser, 2014; Lee, 2010; Rose, 2000; Schauer, 2009, 2022; Savić et al., 2021; Warga, 2004). In this book, I will use *L2 pragmatics*, *second language pragmatics* and *interlanguage pragmatics* interchangeably.[5]

The third subdiscipline of pragmatics relevant to the present investigation is the relatively new subdiscipline of variational pragmatics.

Variational Pragmatics
"Variational pragmatics investigates pragmatic variation in (geographical and social) space [...] [I]n examining pragmatic variation across geographical and social varieties of language, variational pragmatics aims at determining the impact of such factors as region, social class, gender, age and ethnicity on communicative language use. [...] Region in variational pragmatics [...] not only deals with sub-national varieties of a language, but also with languages as pluricentric entities (e.g. German German, Austrian German, Swiss German; English English, Irish English, ...; Argentinian Spanish, Peruvian Spanish, ...)". (Schneider & Barron, 2008, p. 1)

---

[4] In linguistics, second language acquisition (SLA) focuses on learners acquiring an additional language that is not their first language or—in the case of individuals being raised in bilingual or multilingual contexts—one of their first languages. SLA is also the name of a subdiscipline of applied linguistics, and as an umbrella label covers both *second* and *foreign* language acquisition.
[5] While these terms are often used synonymously, Ishihara and Cohen (2022, p. 1) view interlanguage pragmatics as "founded on the conventional native-speaker model", which L2 pragmatics or second language pragmatics does not imply in their opinion.

In variational pragmatics, the concept of pluricentricity is of key importance. According to Clyne (1992, p. 1), "the term pluricentric was employed by Kloss (1978 II: 66–67) to describe languages with several interacting centres, each providing a national variety with at least some of its own codified norms". Many of the languages focused on in this study are pluricentric (e.g., English, French, German, Spanish) and these also tend to be the MFLs that are the most frequently studied languages in secondary settings in the European Union and United States.[6] Thus, being aware of the different norms in countries and regions in which the target language is used is also of great importance for many L2 learners. For example, learners of German ought to know that a greeting which sounds somewhat similar to the German word *Morgen* ("morning") but is used throughout the day—*Moin*—is typically more prevalent in northern Germany and not generally used in southern Germany, Austria or Switzerland. In contrast, the greetings *Grüß Gott* (lit. "Greet God") or *Servus*[7] (from the Latin word for "servant/slave") tend to be used more in southern Germany and Austria. While proficient speakers of German would identify all three expressions as greetings, they might be perceived as unusual outside of the regions that they are typically used in and therefore lead to surprised reactions from interlocutors. Thus, knowing what is considered to be an unmarked greeting (in this case, *Guten Morgen/Tag* "Good morning/day" or *Hallo* "Hello") that can be used widely and in a number of different contexts, compared to one typically used in a particular variety of a language or only in informal conversations, is a topic that ought to be covered in MFL classes, as the first impression in an interaction can impact the remainder of it. Consequently, aspects of variational pragmatics are highly relevant in intercultural language education.

---

[6] Unfortunately, data focusing on higher education, while it would be more relevant in the present study, is not accessible in the same manner as for secondary education. According to EUROSTAT (2022), "English was the most commonly studied foreign language at the upper secondary general […] level in the EU, with 96% […] of students learning it, […], Spanish ranked second (27%), followed by French (22%), German (21%) and Italian (3%)". Data from the American Councils for International Education in 2017 show that the three most frequently studied L2s in the United States were Spanish (69%), French (12%) and German (3%).

[7] Although sometimes translated into English as "at your service" or "your servant", this expression is not considered formal in German and is also used among friends. It can additionally be used as a leave-taking expression. See also DWDS (n.d., 2022).

Like apologies and requests, mentioned in connection with the CCSARP above, greetings are also speech acts. As Bardovi-Harlig (2010, p.219) puts it, "[t]he dominant area of investigation within interlanguage pragmatics has been the speech act". Martínez Flor and Usó Juan (2010, p. 6) agree, and note that "[w]hile it is true that speech act theory is not the whole of pragmatics, this theory has been established as perhaps the most relevant in this field". Roever (2022, p. 10) defines speech acts as "the use of language to accomplish something in the world, or in Austin's (1962) formulation, 'how to do things with words.' Speech acts include such linguistic actions as requesting, apologizing, refusing, suggesting, complaining, criticizing, thanking, complimenting, congratulating, greeting, and others".

How things are done with words in a particular language and culture may vary. This and the effect of cross-cultural differences in the production and comprehension of speech acts is addressed by Ishihara and Cohen (2022, p.11):

> While speech acts are sometimes performed through a single word, phrase, or a sentence (e.g., "Thanks"), in other contexts, they can involve an extended sequence of turns. [...] Realizations of speech acts are often routinized, usually consisting of predictable patterns influenced by shared cultural knowledge. For example, a speaker of American English may say, "Let's get together sometime" as a friendly ritual to signal the end of the conversation without necessarily intending to do so. If a listener comes from another culture where such a statement may be taken as a genuine invitation to schedule a get-together, the interactants may engage in a negotiation of meaning. Because as a result each party may develop (often negative) judgments or stereotypes of the other, it is important that intercultural communicators become aware of potentially different scripts and cultivate an open mind for negotiation.

Since cross-cultural differences in the production and comprehension of speech acts can affect relations between interlocutors negatively,[8] pragmaticians have emphasized the necessity of teaching pragmatics in L2 classes for years. For example, Tatsuki and Houck (2010, p. 1) wrote that "language teachers have long been aware of the devastating effect of learners' grammatically correct, yet situationally inappropriate spoken or written

---

[8] See, for example, Crozet (2015), Félix-Brasdefer (2003) or Paulston (1974).

communication. The study of speech acts [...] offers one resource for addressing some of these instances". In her handbook chapter on pragmatics in instructed second language acquisition, Bardovi-Harlig (2017) addresses the opportunities the teaching of speech acts offers but also mentions other aspects of pragmatics, such as the use of appropriate address terms. This indicates that an L2 learners' pragmatic competence ought not to be solely equated with speech act competence but should be broader, as suggested also in the definition of Ishihara and Cohen (2022).

> **Pragmatic Competence**
> "Pragmatic competence can be viewed as being able to jointly construct meaning through linguistic as well as non-linguistic means within the ongoing interactive context. In a successful meaning-making activity, we understand one another's messages and express ourselves in a socially and contextually preferred manner in order to achieve a particular purpose. For example, expert communicators know just how politely, casually, directly, or indirectly they can best create nuances given the cultural context and its social constraints. Within a culture or community, there is socially acquired and jointly constructed knowledge of more or less acceptable behavior (pragmatic norms) that is negotiated in the local interaction as it unfolds. Rather than being absolutely 'right' or 'wrong,' pragmatic norms are about a range of tendencies or social practices in which certain behaviors are viewed as more or less preferred, suitable, or desirable within the given context. In addition, pragmatic norms vary across languages and cultures or even within a single language, language variety, or culture and can dynamically change over time and across contexts [...]". (Ishihara & Cohen, 2022, p. 2)

Ishihara and Cohen's (2022) definition clearly links pragmatic competence and culture and thus highlights the importance of pragmatic competence for intercultural communication and for L2 learners' intercultural competence. Importantly, it also addresses the link to variational pragmatics and emphasizes that as a result of changes in a culture, pragmatic norms may also change. A recent example for changes on a more global level was the impact of the COVID-19 epidemic on greetings in Germany. While pre-pandemic the handshake was typically used when greeting someone in more formal encounters, this was replaced by a variety of different options during the pandemic, such as nodding, fist or elbow bumps, or shoetip to shoetip touches. This illustrates that pragmatic norms are subject to change and that they are linked to cultural or societal events, which is why the next section focuses on culture.

2.2 Culture

Trosborg (2010, p. 1) argues that "[l]anguage is culture—culture is language. Culture and language are intertwined and shape each other". Yet capturing what culture is and how it can be defined and how it relates to language is not an easy task. This is supported by the views of Spencer-Oatey and Franklin (2009, p. 13), who write that "culture is notoriously difficult to define", and Abrams (2020, p. 9), who notes that defining culture is "a challenging endeavour". To provide a multifaceted view on how culture could be conceptualized, four definitions highlighting different aspects of culture are presented in the box below.

> **Culture**
> "Whereas small *c* culture is commonly understood as referring to phenomena of everyday life, popular cultural products and human behavior, [...] [b]ig *C* Culture is conceived as manifesting itself in ideas, values, history, institutions, literature, philosophy and artistic products". (Sercu, 2000, p. 28)
> "Probably the most popular explanation of the notion of culture is [...] *a comparison of culture to an iceberg* only the tip of which is visible (language, food, appearance, etc.) whereas a large part of the iceberg is difficult to see or grasp (communication style, beliefs, values, attitudes, perceptions, etc.). The items in the invisible body of the iceberg include a long list of notions from definitions of beauty or respect to patterns of group decision making, ideals governing child-raising, as well as values relating to leadership, prestige, health, love or death (Lussier et al. 2007)". (Jedynak, 2011, p. 65; my emphasis)
> "[D]istinctions can be drawn between the material, social and subjective aspects of culture. Material culture consists of the physical artefacts which are commonly used by the members of a cultural

(continued)

> (continued)
> group (e.g. the tools, goods, foods, clothing, etc.); social culture consists of the social institutions of the group (e.g., the language, religion, laws, rules of social conduct, folklore, cultural icons, etc.); and subjective culture consists of the beliefs, norms, collective memories, attitudes, values, discourses and practices which group members commonly use as a frame of reference for thinking about, making sense of and relating to the world. Culture itself is a composite formed from all three aspects—it consists of a network of material, social and subjective resources. The total set of cultural resources is distributed across the entire group, but each individual member of the group appropriates and uses only a subset of the total set of cultural resources potentially available to them". (CoE, 2014, pp. 13–14)
>
> "Culture is not simply a body of knowledge, but a framework in which people live their lives, communicate and interpret shared meanings, and select possible actions to achieve goals. Seen in this way, it becomes fundamentally necessary to engage with the variability inherent in any culture. This involves a movement away from the idea of a national culture to recognize that culture varies with time, place, and social category, and for age, gender, religion, ethnicity and sexuality (Norton, 2000). […] People can resist, subvert or challenge the cultural practices to which they are exposed to in their first and in additional cultures they acquire. […] Culture in this sense is dynamic, evolving and not easily summarized for teaching; it is the complexity of culture with which the learner must engage". (Liddicoat & Scarino, 2013, pp. 32)

The definitions by Sercu (2000) and Jedynak (2011) are somewhat similar in that they contrast observable aspects of culture, such as behaviour and language, with other aspects that may be less obvious to newcomers to a particular culture and may necessitate deeper engagement with a culture's history, beliefs, norms and artistic products in order to understand them. These aspects may require a deeper knowledge of the target culture and potentially also a higher proficiency in the language(s) spoken by members of the culture. Different greeting expressions used in everyday service encounter interactions may be easy to observe and learn, whereas linguistic and behavioural taboos, intertextual references to valued artistic products, and positive or negative stereotypes towards institutions may be more difficult for L2 learners to understand, therefore, requiring more cultural background knowledge and potentially also a higher proficiency in the L2.

The definitions of culture from the Council of Europe (2014) and Liddicoat and Scarino (2013) highlight the important point that culture is not monolithic and static but rather that much variation and diversity exists, that culture is subject to change and that individuals tend to choose aspects of culture that relate to their identity. These aspects of culture are also highly relevant for MFL educators, since they have an impact on what they teach and which materials they select (see also Chap. 5). I still vividly remember a seminar on spoken language that I attended during my MA studies at the University of Nottingham over 20 years ago in which Rebecca Hughes shared a discussion she had with a colleague about including youth language in a language course. They discussed whether including youth language was a good idea or not, since expressions used by teenagers of a particular generation may fall out of use quickly and may not be widely understood nor suitable for a variety of different contexts. This has stayed with me ever since, and I frequently reflect on it when encountering innovations in language use, such as gender-neutral language in German (see, e.g., Diewald & Steinhauer, 2017, 2020) or pragmatic features of a particular variety of English that I had not come across before, such as the "will I" routine for the speech act of offering in Irish English (see Barron, 2005). The question that arises for language learners and language teachers alike is: which aspects of culture do L2 learners need to know in order to successfully navigate interactions in their MFL?

While youth language—due to its often-transient nature—may either not feature in language classes at all or may receive only limited attention, aspects of language that are frequently encountered in particular varieties of the target language and which differ from the language use in other varieties may be rather important. For example, the "will I" offer routine in Irish English may be highly relevant for L2 learners of English planning to study or work in Ireland, but less so for others who are more likely to interact more with speakers of other English varieties. Decisions also need to be taken with regard to obsolete features of language, such as the use of *pray* as a synonym of *please* in English (see Busse, 2008; Lutzky & Demmen, 2013) or the term of address *Fräulein* in German, which was used for unmarried females and abolished in official government language in Germany in 1972, being replaced by the term *Frau*, now used for all adult females (Kotthoff & Nübling, 2018).

Learning about the different meanings of *pray* may be essential for students of English who are going to encounter Shakespeare and work with historic language but may be of little relevance for university students taking English classes as part of their international relations degree. While *Fräulein* has fallen out of use, it may be important for learners of German whose own first language (L1) still has different terms of address for females based on their marital status: for L2 learners of German with this background, it may be helpful to know that equivalent German address terms once existed but are no longer in use, as this can help prevent negative transfer[9] from their L1 and so prevent the learner from causing offence.[10] Societal and political changes resulting in changes in the way the language is used in a specific culture tie in closely with Liddicoat and Scarino's (2013) definition of culture as dynamic and evolving. While something may have been acceptable or in accordance with the law a few years or decades ago, that may no longer be the case today.

Pragmaticians have argued for years that inappropriate, impolite and offensive language ought to be addressed in MFL classrooms (e.g., House, 2015; Morollón Martí, 2022; Mugford, 2008, 2019). Providing MFL learners with information on what may be considered rude or inappropriate in a language and culture can help L2 learners better understand their interlocutors' moods and emotions. If MFL learners know what is considered to be inappropriate or impolite in a particular culture (see Schauer, 2017, on differences in the perception of inappropriateness and impoliteness), they can not only avoid using language that may cause offence but

---

[9] In SLA, two types of transfer are commonly distinguished: negative and positive. In the case of positive transfer, norms or linguistic features from an L2 learner's native language can be taken and (perhaps in a slightly modified form) reused in the L2 because the meaning and use is very similar: for example, the greeting *hallo* (German), *hello* (English) and *hallå* (Swedish); or *airport* (English) and *aeroporto* (Italian). Negative transfer occurs when the norms or linguistic features from an L2 learner's native language do not match with those of the target language: for example, *Henne* in German ("hen", a female farmyard animal) and *henne* in Swedish ("her", personal pronoun); or *I am 12 years old* in English and *ho dodici anni* in Italian (lit. "I have 12 years"). Pairs of similar words with different meanings across languages that are likely to lead to negative transfer are sometimes referred to as false friends.

[10] As mentioned in a discussion of cross-cultural differences in address terms in Schauer (2019, p. 137), a male learner of German whose L1 had different terms of address for females based on marital status used *Fräulein* to address a young German female a few years ago. This was not at all well received by his interlocutor and illustrates that even obsolete language may still need to be taught in order to make learners aware that these language forms are no longer appropriate.

they are also better prepared for conflict and potentially dangerous situations if this language is directed towards them.

Swear words and taboo language are overt examples of impolite language. Ludwig and Summer (2023, p. 13) argue in their edited volume on taboos and controversial topics in L2 education that "taboos are a key element of every culture [and that] they can be explored to identify cultural similarities and differences". While some swear words, such as the "F-word", are also used in countries in which English is not the L1, such as in Germany and Sweden, and could therefore be considered intercultural, the use of other swear words tends to be more culturally and temporally specific (e.g., Ljung, 2011), thus necessitating knowledge of the respective culture's norms. For example, Dewaele (2015) found that the use of swear words differs in American and British English. In a later study, Dewaele (2016) compared the perceived offensiveness of specific English expressions and found that English native speakers and English L2 learners' perceptions differed with regard to their severity. This further indicates that L2 learners may benefit from instruction on the linguistic manifestations of culture, such as swear words and taboo expressions.

2.3 Communicative Competence

Another essential concept in MFL education that is relevant for this study is communicative competence. Thornbury (2016, p. 224) refers to a "seismic shift" in the field of L2 language teaching in the 1970s, when researchers and educators who were dissatisfied with the results of the predominantly language structure-based teaching approaches that had dominated MFL classrooms until then developed a new functional approach called communicative language teaching.[11] This new approach was closely tied to the concept of communicative competence, which "has informed the field of second language acquisition for approximately 50 years" (Kanwit & Solon, 2023, p. 1).

---

[11] According to Hummel (2014, p. 115), communicative language teaching refers to "an approach that emphasizes using techniques that engage learners in the pragmatic, authentic, functional use of language for meaningful purposes". The connection to pragmatics is not only mentioned by Hummel but also by others. When discussing communicative language teaching, Larsen-Freeman and Anderson (2011, p. 115) highlight the necessity of appropriate language use and, referring to Wilkins (1976), state that "learners needed to perform certain functions, such as promising, inviting and declining invitations", thereby again demonstrating the close link between communicative language teaching and pragmatics.

In one of the earliest definitions of communicative competence—deliberately included in both an English and a German language version in a book that is written in German but focuses on teaching English as a foreign language—Piepho (1974, p. 132) writes that "[c]ommunicative competence comprises the capacities of a speaker/learner to realize communicative performance and communicative discourse, i.e. the ability to identify the meanings and purposes of messages as well as the ability to convey meaning and make oneself understood". What is interesting about Piepho's book is that it frequently refers to pragmatics, at a time when interlanguage pragmatics was still very much in its infancy. This demonstrates, however, that some researchers in the field of language education saw the potential of pragmatics as component of communicative competence very early on. Although the first books and articles addressing communicative competence were published in the 1970s (e.g., Savignon, 1976), and some of these also explicitly addressed inappropriate language choices and the effects of perceived impolite behaviour (see, e.g., Paulston, 1974, on cross-cultural differences between Swedish and American English), pragmatics was not explicitly referred to in all the communicative competence frameworks that were subsequently developed by researchers in English language teaching (ELT) and second language acquisition (SLA), particularly in some of the ones that received a great deal of attention (e.g., Canale & Swain, 1980). Notably, however, models of communicative competence developed by linguists in the field of language testing tended to refer to pragmatics from the early 1980s (e.g., Bachman, 1990; Bachman & Palmer, 1982, 2010).

To lay the foundation for intercultural competence models, which can include components of communicative competence models, it is necessary to take a more detailed look at the components of communicative competence models. The major components of Canale and Swain's (1980, pp. 29–31) model were grammatical competence (including morphology, syntax, semantics and phonology), sociolinguistic competence (including sociocultural and discourse rules)[12] and strategic competence ("verbal and

---

[12] Although it is never explicitly mentioned in the text, Canale and Swain's sociocultural rules could cover the area of pragmatics, since they write that the "primary focus of these rules is on the extent to which certain propositions and communicative functions are appropriate within a given sociocultural context depending on contextual factors such as topic, role of participants, setting, and norms of interaction" (1983, p. 30).

nonverbal communication strategies that may be called into action to compensate for breakdowns in communication"). In 1983, Canale presented a revised version of the earlier framework he developed with Swain, in which grammatical competence remains the same and strategic competence is proposed to also cover strategies to enhance the effectiveness of communication (e.g., changing the volume of one's voice). The discourse aspect of sociolinguistic competence is extracted from sociolinguistic competence and raised to an independent element on par with the others, resulting in four communicative competence components in Canale (1983) instead of three in Canale and Swain (1980). Sociolinguistic competence now only refers to "the extent to which utterances are produced and understood appropriately in different sociolinguistic contexts depending on contextual factors such as status of the participants, purposes of the interaction and norms of convention of interaction. Appropriateness [...] refers to both appropriateness of meaning and appropriateness of form" (Canale, 1983, p. 7). The link to pragmatics is also established in the further discussion of the revised sociolinguistic competence component in which pragmatic rules are mentioned.

Like the frameworks by Canale and Swain (1980) and Canale (1983), Bachman and Palmer's original communicative competence model (1982) also includes a grammatical competence component (including morphology and syntax), as well as pragmatic (covering vocabulary, cohesion and organization) and sociolinguistic components (including register, nativeness and non-literal language). This model was then subjected to a construct validation study resulting in a rearrangement of some components and subsequent revised frameworks,[13] such as Bachman's (1990) model that includes the major components of organizational competence (comprising grammatical competence and textual competence) and pragmatic competence (comprising illocutionary competence and sociolinguistic competence) and Bachman and Palmer's (2010) model that features the major components of language competence (consisting of organizational and pragmatic knowledge) and strategic competence.

This overview of different communicative competence models thus shows that there is no universal agreement on all of the components of

---

[13] While the revised models are not all labelled as models of communicative competence, they are generally considered to refer to it and are therefore treated as such in the literature.

communicative competence nor on the terminology that is used to refer to specific linguistic phenomena, such as appropriateness and politeness. Consequently, developers of intercultural communicative competence frameworks that include aspects of communicative competence need to define what they consider these components to be, since no assumptions can be made based on the varying definitions of communicative competence in the literature.

2.4 Intercultural (Communicative) Competence

As Jackson (2019, p. 479) notes, "intercultural competence is a difficult construct to pin down and over the years scholars have put forward numerous definitions". One of the difficulties with pinning it down is that *intercultural competence* is a technical term that has been used in a variety of different academic disciplines, such as business studies, health care research, social work studies and tourism studies (cf. Deardorff, 2009; Schauer, 2016), which all have their very specific subject-based perspectives on what the concept ought to entail or not, resulting in rather different models and components featured in these models. For example, Spitzberg and Changnon (2009) found more than 300 components that are related to intercultural competence in their overview study. While some models of intercultural competence are also rather vague[14] with regard to linguistic aspects of intercultural competence (see also Arasaratnam- Smith 2017), others focus more on these (e.g., Byram, 1997, 2009; Fantini, 2019) and are therefore also more relevant to the present investigation.

Another difficulty has to do with the precise term used, since some scholars refer to "intercultural competence" in early publications and then subsequently refer to "intercultural communicative competence" (ICC),[15]

---

[14] This is supported by McConachy and Liddicoat (2022, p. 4) who note that

> in many models of constructs such as intercultural competence or intercultural communicative competence, reference to language is often omitted or is considered somewhat generically as part of communication. This invisibility of languages in theorizing about intercultural communication renders the task of connecting language and intercultural competence more difficult.

[15] In this book, I will be using IC as an acronym for intercultural competence and ICC as an acronym for intercultural communicative competence.

seemingly using the two terms as synonyms (see Schauer, 2022), while other researchers have distinct definitions for the two terms that delineate the differences (e.g., Byram, 2009, 2021).

A third difficulty is that, apart from the two aforementioned terms, other terms may be used to refer to the same concept or similar ones. For example, Spencer-Oatey (2010) and Jackson (2019) list the following possibilities: cross-cultural adjustment, cross-cultural awareness, cross-cultural or intercultural effectiveness, intercultural communication competence, global mindset, and transcultural (communication) competence. Braun et al. (2020) argue that diversity competence is also used as a synonym. As Spencer-Oatey (2010, p. 189) noted early on when reviewing the different terms that had been suggested, "there does not seem to be any consistent distinction between these various terms".

The complexity and variability of the term means that intercultural (communicative) competence may mean many different things to many different people (e.g., researchers, educators and curriculum developers). The present study hopes to shed some light on what teachers of MFLs in higher education consider intercultural competence to be and how it relates to pragmatics.[16]

One of the scholars associated with intercultural (communicative) competence who was mentioned above and who is frequently referred to in publications focusing on L2 language learning and teaching is Michael Byram. Jackson (2019, p. 482) writes that "Byram's (1997) model of intercultural communicative competence has had a major impact on intercultural pedagogy and second/foreign language teaching, especially in Europe". In contrast to some researchers who have developed models of IC or ICC, Byram has always been very clear about how he differentiates the two terms.

---

[16] Due to space constraints, the following discussion centres on the ICC models by Byram (1997, 2009, 2021) and Fantini (2019). For publications that address specific aspects of intercultural competence and pragmatics, see, for example, Liddicoat (2014) and McConachy and Liddicoat (2016) on pragmatics and intercultural mediation or McConachy (2022) on pragmatic awareness and intercultural learning.

> **Intercultural Competence (Byram's, 1997 Definition)**
> "Individuals have the ability to interact *in their own language* with people from another country and culture, drawing upon their knowledge about intercultural communication, their attitudes of interest in otherness, and their skills in interpreting, relating and discovering, i.e., of overcoming and enjoying intercultural contact". (Byram, 1997, p. 70; my emphasis)

> **Intercultural Communicative Competence (Byram's, 1997 Definition)**
> "[Intercultural communicative competence is the ability] to interact with people from another country and culture *in a foreign language*. [Individuals who have this competence] are able to negotiate a mode of communication and interaction which is satisfactory to themselves and the other and they are able to act as mediator between people of different cultural origins. Their knowledge of another culture is linked to their language competence through their ability to use language appropriately—sociolinguistic and discourse competence—and their awareness of the specific meanings, values and connotations of the language". (Byram, 1997, p. 71; my emphasis)

Thus, according to Byram (1997), the key difference between IC and ICC is whether an individual's first or foreign language is used. While intercultural competence refers to skills that are needed in intercultural interactions in which an individual communicates in their first or native language, intercultural communicative competence comprises competencies that are necessary when the individual uses a foreign language in intercultural interactions. Figure 2.1 presents his model of IC and ICC. However, it needs to be noted that Byram's schematic presentation of his model has changed over the years. The schematic illustration of the model included here represents the most recent version from 2021 and differs in some respects from earlier versions, such as those found in Byram (1997, 2009).

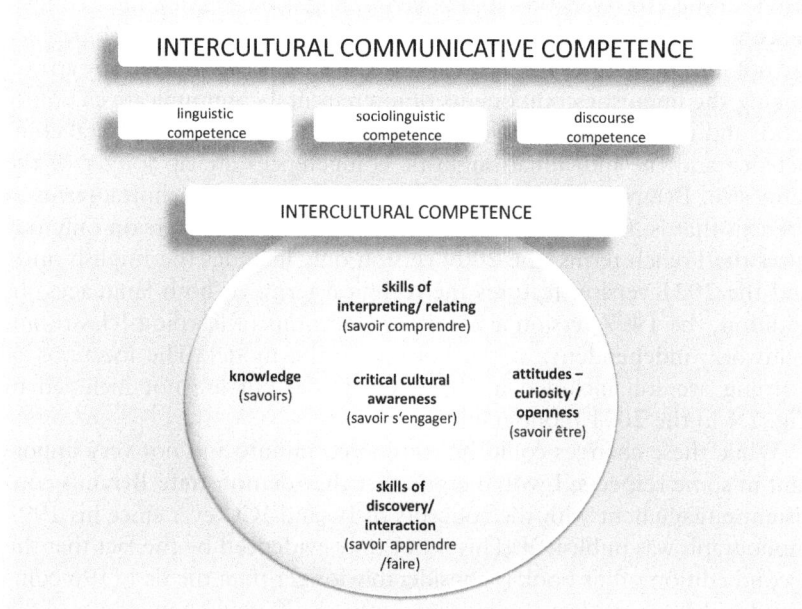

Fig. 2.1 Byram's (2021) model of intercultural competence and intercultural communicative competence

In the original 1997 version,[17] the three linguistic components (linguistic, sociolinguistic and discourse competence) and intercultural competence are of the same size and connected via bidirectional arrows. However, while intercultural competence is linked to all three linguistic competences, the individual linguistic competences are not all linked in the 1997 model. In that model, sociolinguistic competence is at the centre—as it

---

[17] It needs to be noted that Byram's 1997 monograph only includes one schematic illustration of ICC models provided on page 73. This illustration is only referred to as "Figure 3.1" and thus has no caption outlining the content. In contrast, in the 2009 version, the model presented on page 323 is referred to as "Figure 18.1 A model of intercultural communicative competence". The 2021 monograph features two schematic illustrations, "Figure 2.1 Intercultural competence and intercultural communicative competence" on page 62, which is similar to the 2009 figure, and "Figure 3.1 Intercultural communicative competence and locations of learning" on page 98, which is similar to the 1997 figure. In my discussion here I refer to the only figure included in 1997, that is, Figure 3.1, Figure 18.1 in the 2009 publication and Figure 2.1 in the 2021 publication.

also is in the 2021 version—and linked to linguistic and discourse competence with bidirectional arrows; but linguistic and discourse competence are not linked. Neither the 2009 nor the 2021 versions include any arrows linking the linguistic components of intercultural communicative competence and intercultural competence, and the boxes for intercultural competence and the individual linguistic competences are no longer of the same size. Byram's model is also famous for his use of technical terms in French, that is, the different savoirs. The original 1997 version only features the French terms, the 2009 version only includes the English ones, and the 2021 version features the technical terms in both languages. In addition, the 1997 version also features locations of learning (classroom, fieldwork, independent) at the bottom of the model. The locations of learning are still included in the 2009 model but are not included in Fig. 2.1 in the 2021 monograph.

While these changes could be considered minute and not very important in some respects, I would argue that they demonstrate Byram's consistent engagement with the concepts of IC and ICC ever since his 1997 monograph was published. This is not only evidenced by the fact that the second edition of his book is considerably longer than the first (196 compared to 124 pages) but also by comments on different components of the model. Although the definitions for the three linguistic competences remain largely the same—apart from some very minor stylistic changes—his 2021 book features a very long footnote addressing pronunciation; as Byram notes, he did not discuss this in his 1997 book at all.

Byram's definitions of the three linguistic competences are based on van Ek (1986) and are presented here from the most recent version (Byram, 2021, p. 84).

Linguistic competence	The ability to apply knowledge of the rules of a standard version of the language to produce and interpret spoken and written language [this is accompanied by the aforementioned long footnote on pronunciation].
Sociolinguistic competence	The ability to give to the language produced by an interlocutor—whether native speaker or not—meanings which are taken for granted by the interlocutor or which are negotiated and made explicit with the interlocutor.
Discourse competence	The ability to use, discover and negotiate strategies for the production and interpretation of monologic[18] or dialogic texts which follow the conventions of the culture of an interlocutor or are negotiated as intercultural texts for particular purposes.

[18] As mentioned above, the 2021 version features some minor stylistic changes compared to the 1997 original. This is one of them, since the 1997 refers to "monologue or dialogue texts" instead (p. 48).

What is noteworthy here is the absence of pragmatic competence. However, this is not surprising; as Spencer-Oatey (2010, p. 189) noted, "in nearly all […] [intercultural competence] frameworks, communication is highlighted as being of crucial importance, yet there is very rarely any mention in these other disciplines of pragmatics research into intercultural interaction, despite the large amount that has been carried out". While the term *pragmatics* is rarely used unambiguously in Byram's (2021) monograph,[19] aspects that are relevant from a pragmatic competence perspective are already present in several components of Byram's 1997 model, such as "knowledge of the processes of social interaction in one's interlocutor's country" and "readiness to engage with conventions and rites of verbal and non-verbal communication and interaction" (Byram, 1997, pp. 50–51). It is regrettable that his 2021 monograph does not address pragmatics in more detail, but perhaps future articles or editions of the book will do so.

Another important scholar who has written on intercultural (communicative) competence and is often referred to by linguists working in this area (e.g., Jackson, 2019; Schauer 2016, 2021; Spencer-Oatey 2010) is Alvino Fantini, who explicitly addressed the link between foreign language learning and intercultural competence in his early publications:

> How effective and appropriate can an individual be in an intercultural context with—and without—ability in the target language? (cf. Kealey, 1990). Notions of "effectiveness" and "appropriateness" help to suggest two views of the issue. Whereas effectiveness is often a judgment from one's own perspective, appropriateness is clearly based on judgments from the host perspective. Although communication across cultures may occur in one's own language (especially where English or another dominant language is involved), there is a qualitative difference between communicating in one's own language and/or in the language of one's hosts. Whichever the case, second language (L2) proficiency is critical to functioning effectively and appropriately in cross-cultural situations, plus the added benefit that exposure to a second linguaculture (LC2) affords an opportunity to develop a different or at least, an expanded, vision of the world. Needless to say, developing an LC3 or LC4 is even better in that it demands reconfiguring the polarization that commonly occurs in the experience of the bilingual-bicultural individual. (Fantini, 1995, p. 150)

---

[19] As I have observed previously, "it needs to be noted that pragmatics as a technical term rarely features unambiguously in Byram's 1997 monograph, that is, when the term occurs, it is not always clear whether it is used in a technical sense or as a synonym of 'sensible'" (Schauer, 2022, p. 176).

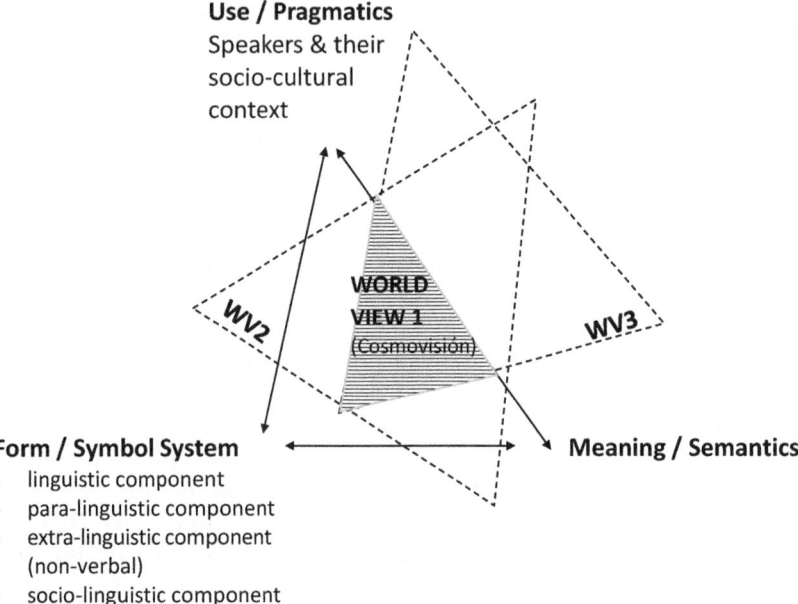

Fig. 2.2 Fantini's (1995) conceptualization of the link between world view and language

Thus, like Byram (1997, 2021), Fantini also considers intercultural communication occurring in an individual's first language but highlights the importance of proficiency in additional languages. Central to Fantini's early considerations of IC are the world views of interlocutors, which he also presented in a figure that indicates distinct and overlapping areas of world views, presented here as Fig. 2.2. This figure is interesting because it indicates how Fantini sees the interrelationships between the various linguistic components and world views of interlocutors. In addition, the figure features pragmatics and thus illustrates the relevance of pragmatics for individuals' world views and the broader field of IC.

Fantini's 1995 article alludes to a possible definition of IC but does not actually spell it out. This is done in one of his later publications (Fantini, 2009) that also takes up the key notions of *appropriateness* and *effectiveness* that he discussed in his 1995 article.

Intercultural Competence (Fantini's, 2009 Definition)
"Each individual possesses a native communicative competence (CC_1) and, during intercultural contact, encounters that of one's interlocutor (CC_2). Those who choose to acquire a second communicative competence, CC_2, develop intercultural competence. Intercultural competence, then, acknowledges the presence of CC_1 and the development of CC_2 and, in addition, the insights that derive from now being in a position to compare and contrast both. This unique vantage point is an important aspect of intercultural competence and something that a monolingual, monocultural native of either system cannot possibly access.

Stated another way, intercultural competence may be defined as complex abilities that are required to perform *effectively* and *appropriately* when interacting with others who are linguistically and culturally different from oneself. Whereas *effective* reflects the view of one's own performance in the target language culture (LC_2; i.e., an outsiders or 'etic' view), *appropriate* reflects how natives perceive such performance (i.e., an insider's or 'emic' view)". (Fantini, 2009, p. 458)

Since the terms *effective* and *appropriate* are frequently used to describe pragmatic competence (e.g., Félix-Brasdefer, 2019; Levey, 2017; Ninio & Snow, 1996; Taguchi, 2017), the link between intercultural competence and pragmatics seems obvious when Fantini's definition for IC is used. Unfortunately, however, like Byram (1997, 2021), Fantini (1995) does not discuss the connection between IC and pragmatics more explicitly. This absence of explicit links in the publications of two authors who are frequently referred to in the field of intercultural (communicative) competence and language education is one of the reasons why this book was written.

In a 2019 publication, Fantini includes a schematic illustration of what intercultural communicative competence is, based on an analysis of "over 200 publications, in several languages, spanning half a century" (Fantini, 2019, p. 38). In this model, intercultural communicative competence is positioned at the top with arrows leading to five main features located at positions below ICC. From left to right these main features are: (1)

characteristics/attributes, (2) target language proficiency, (3) a longitudinal, developmental process, (4) dimensions and (5) abilities. Three of the main features (characteristics/attributes, dimensions, and abilities), contain sub-features. For (1) characteristics/attributes these are: "open-minded, patience, motivation, interested, empathy, self-reliance, sense of humour, clear sense of self, flexibility/adaptability, relativity, tolerance for differences, perceptiveness, suspend judgement, tolerance for ambiguity [as well as several unnamed] others" (p. 38). The sub-features of dimensions are "knowledge, attitudes/affect, skills and awareness", while abilities include the subfeatures "establish relationships, communicate well and collaborate" (p. 38).

Some features of Fantini's model are similar to Byram's, 1997 model; for example, "open-minded" is parallel to Byram's "openness". In addition, both models include a "knowledge" feature. However, whereas Byram lists components of communicative competence, Fantini (2019) refers to target language proficiency—thereby echoing the point he made in his 1995 publication regarding its relevance—and highlights the process, thus supporting the well-known process model of Deardorff (2006).[20]

While it is important to know the views of scholars researching IC and ICC, since their work often lays the foundation of curricula, influences policy decisions and impacts teacher training programmes, I also believe that is important to find out what frontline teaching staff think about IC and ICC. This was another reason why this book was written. The following chapter begins with this task by providing detailed information on the present study and its participants.

REFERENCES

Abrams, Z. (2020). *Intercultural communication and language pedagogy*. Cambridge University Press.
Achiba, M. (2003). *Learning to request in a second language*. Multilingual Matters.
American Councils for International Education. (2017). *Language research—FLE—State of language in the US*. https://www.americancouncils.org/language-research-fle-state-language-us

---

[20] Since Deardorff is not a linguist and her model was developed from a different disciplinary perspective, it will not be discussed here. For more detailed discussions of her work, see Deardorff (2006), Deardorff and Arasaratnam-Smith (2017) or Arasaratnam-Smith and Deardorff (2022).

Arasaratnam- Smith, L. A. (2017). Intercultural competence – An overview. In D. K. Deardorff & L. A. Arasaratnam- Smith (Eds.), *Intercultural competence in higher education: International approaches, assessment, application* (pp. 7–18). Routledge.
Arasaratnam-Smith, L. A., & Deardorff, D. K. (Eds.). (2022). *Developing intercultural competence in higher education: International students' stories and self-reflection.* Routledge.
Aslan, E. (2021). Perceptions of pragmatics in EIL: Voices from scholars and teachers. In Z. Tajeddin & M. Alemi (Eds.), *Pragmatics pedagogy in English as an international language* (pp. 172–190). Routledge.
Bachman, L. F. (1990). *Fundamental considerations in language testing.* Oxford University Press.
Bachman, L. F., & Palmer, A. S. (1982). The construct validation of some components of communicative proficiency. *TESOL Quarterly, 16*(4), 449–465. https://doi.org/10.2307/3586464
Bachman, L. F., & Palmer, A. S. (2010). *Language assessment in practice: Developing language assessments and justifying their use in the real world.* Oxford University Press.
Bardovi-Harlig, K. (2010). Exploring the pragmatics of interlanguage pragmatics: Definition by design. In A. Trosborg (Ed.), *Pragmatics across languages and cultures* (pp. 219–260). De Gruyter Mouton.
Bardovi-Harlig, K. (2013). Developing L2 pragmatics. *Language Learning, 63*(1), 68–86.
Bardovi-Harlig, K. (2017). Acquisition of L2 pragmatics. In S. Loewen & M. Sato (Eds.), *The Routledge handbook of instructed second language acquisition* (pp. 224–245). Routledge.
Barron, A. (2003). *Acquisition in interlanguage pragmatics: How to do things with words in a study abroad context.* John Benjamins.
Barron, A. (2005). Offering in Ireland and England. In A. Barron & K. P. Schneider (Eds.), *The pragmatics of Irish English* (pp. 141–177). Walter de Gruyter.
Barron, A., Gu, Y., & Steen, G. (2017). Pragmatics broadly viewed: Introduction. In A. Barron, Y. Gu, & G. Steen (Eds.), *The Routledge handbook of pragmatics* (pp. 1–4). Routledge.
Bataineh, R. F., & Bataineh, R. F. (2008). A cross-cultural comparison of apologies by native speakers of American English and Jordanian Arabic. *Journal of Pragmatics, 40*(4), 792–821.
Blum-Kulka, S., House, J., & Kasper, G. (1989). *Cross-cultural pragmatics: Requests and apologies.* Ablex.
Braun, E., Spexard, A., Nowakowski, A., & Hannover, B. (2020). Self-assessment of diversity competence as part of regular teaching evaluations in higher education: Raising awareness for diversity issues. *Tertiary Education and Management, 26*, 171–183.

Busse, U. (2008). An inventory of directives in Shakespeare's King Lear. In A. H. Jucker & I. Taavitsainen (Eds.), *Speech acts in the history of English* (pp. 85–114). John Benjamins.

Byram, M. (1997). *Teaching and assessing intercultural communicative competence*. Multilingual Matters.

Byram, M. (2009). Intercultural speaker and the pedagogy of foreign language education. In D. Deardorff (Ed.), *The SAGE handbook of intercultural competence* (pp. 321–332). Sage.

Byram, M. (2021). *Teaching and assessing intercultural communicative competence revisited* (2nd ed.). Multilingual Matters.

Canale, M. (1983). From communicative competence to communicative language pedagogy. In J. C. Richards & R. W. Schmidt (Eds.), *Language and communication* (pp. 2–27). Longman.

Canale, M., & Swain, M. (1980). Theoretical bases of communicative approaches to second language teaching and testing. *Applied Linguistics, 1*(1), 1–47.

Celce-Murcia, M., & Olshtain, E. (2000). *Discourse and contexts in language teaching: A guide for language teachers*. Cambridge University Press.

Chen, Y., Chen, C., & Chang, M. (2011). American and Chinese complaints: Strategy use from a cross-cultural perspective. *Intercultural Pragmatics, 8*(2), 253–275.

Clyne, M. (1992). Pluricentric languages: An introduction. In M. Clyne (Ed.), *Pluricentric languages: Differing norms in different nations* (pp. 1–10). Mouton de Gruyter.

Council of Europe. (2014). *Developing intercultural competence through education*. Council of Europe Publishing.

Crozet, C. (2015). On language and interculturality: Teaching languages and cultures for a global world. In J. C. H. Lee (Ed.), *Narratives of globalisation – Reflecting on the global condition* (pp. 85–94). Rowan & Littlefield International.

Crystal, D. (1985). *A dictionary of linguistics and phonetics* (2nd ed.). Blackwell.

Culpeper, J., & Schauer, G. A. (2018). Pragmatics. In J. Culpeper, F. Katamba, P. Kerswill, T. McEnery, & R. Wodak (Eds.), *English language: Description, variation and use* (2nd ed., pp. 146–164). Palgrave.

Culpeper, J., Marti, L., Mei, M., Nevala, M., & Schauer, G. A. (2010). Cross-cultural variation in the perception of impoliteness: A study of impoliteness events reported by students in England, China, Finland, Germany and Turkey. *Intercultural Pragmatics, 7*(4), 597–624.

Culpeper, J., Mackey, A., & Taguchi, N. (2018). *Second language pragmatics – From theory to research*. Routledge.

Deardorff, D. K. (2006). Identification and assessment of intercultural competence as a student outcome of internationalization. *Journal of Studies in International Education, 10*(3), 241–266.

Deardorff, D. K. (Ed.). (2009). *The SAGE handbook of intercultural competence*. Sage.
Deardorff, D. K., & Arasaratnam-Smith, L. A. (2017). *Intercultural competence in higher education: International approaches, assessment and application*. Routledge.
Dewaele, J. M. (2015). British "bollocks" versus American "jerk": Do native British English speakers swear more—Or differently—Compared to American English speakers? *Applied Linguistics Review, 6*(3), 309–339.
Dewaele, J. M. (2016). Thirty shades of offensiveness: L1 and LX English users' understanding, perception and self-reported use of negative emotion-laden words. *Journal of Pragmatics, 94*, 112–127.
Diewald, G., & Steinhauer, A. (2017). *Richtig gendern: Wie Sie angemessen und verständlich schreiben*. Duden Verlag.
Diewald, G., & Steinhauer, A. (2020). *Handbuch geschlechtergerechte Sprache: Wie Sie angemessen und verständlich gendern*. Duden Verlag.
DWDS. (2022, November 7). *Zur Begrüßung: Hallo—Servus—ciao*. Digitales Wörterbuch der deutschen Sprache. https://www.dwds.de/b/zur-begruessung-hallo-servus-ciao/
DWDS. (n.d.). Servus. In *Digitales Wörterbuch der deutschen Sprache*. Retrieved April 13, 2023, from https://www.dwds.de/wb/Servus
EUROSTAT. (2022, 23 September). *What languages are studied the most in the EU?* https://ec.europa.eu/eurostat/de/web/products-eurostat-news/-/ddn-20220923-1#
Fantini, A. E. (1995). Introduction—Language, culture and world view: Exploring the nexus. *International Journal of Intercultural Relations, 19*(2), 143–153.
Fantini, A. E. (2009). Assessing intercultural competence: Issues and tools. In D. K. Deardorff (Ed.), *The SAGE handbook of intercultural competence* (pp. 456–476). Sage.
Fantini, A. E. (2019). *Intercultural communicative competence in educational exchange: A multinational perspective*. Routledge.
Félix-Brasdefer, J. C. (2003). Declining an invitation: A cross-cultural study of pragmatic strategies in American English and Latin American Spanish. *Multilingua, 22*(3), 225–255.
Félix-Brasdefer, J. C. (2007). Pragmatic development in the Spanish as a FL classroom: A cross-sectional study of learner requests. *Intercultural Pragmatics, 4*(2), 253–286.
Félix-Brasdefer, J. C. (2019). Speech acts in interaction: Negotiating joint action in a second language. In N. Taguchi (Ed.), *The Routledge handbook of second language acquisition and pragmatics* (pp. 17–30). Routledge.
Félix-Brasdefer, J. C., & Shively, R. (2021). Introduction. In J. C. Félix-Brasdefer & R. Shively (Eds.), *New directions in second language pragmatics* (pp. 1–10). De Gruyter Mouton.

Glaser, K. (2014). Inductive or deductive? The impact of the method of instruction on the acquisition of pragmatic competence in EFL. .
House, J. (2015). Epilogue: Impoliteness in learning and teaching. In B. Pizziconi & M. A. Locher (Eds.), *Teaching and learning (im)politeness* (pp. 247–254). De Gruyter.
House, J., & Kádár, D. (2021). *Cross-cultural pragmatics*. Cambridge University Press.
Hummel, K. M. (2014). *Introducing second language acquisition: Perspectives and practices*. Wiley Blackwell.
Ishihara, N., & Cohen, A. D. (2022). *Teaching and learning pragmatics: Where language and culture meet* (2nd ed.). Routledge.
Jackson, J. (2019). Intercultural competence and L2 pragmatics. In N. Taguchi (Ed.), *The Routledge handbook of second language acquisition and pragmatics* (pp. 479–494). Routledge.
Jedynak, M. (2011). The attitudes of English language teachers towards developing intercultural communicative competence. In J. Arabski & A. Wojtaszek (Eds.), *Aspects of culture in second language acquisition and foreign language learning* (pp. 63–76). Springer.
Jucker, A. H. (2012). Pragmatics in the history of linguistic thought. In K. Allan & K. M. Jaszczolt (Eds.), *The Cambridge handbook of pragmatics* (pp. 495–512). Cambridge University Press.
Kanwit, M., & Solon, M. (2023). Introduction: Historical overview, key constructs, and recent developments in the study of communicative competence. In M. Kanwit & M. Solon (Eds.), *Communicative competence in a second language: Theory, method and applications* (pp. 1–18). Routledge.
Kotthoff, H., & Nübling, D. (2018). Genderlinguistik: Eine Einführung in Sprache, Gespräch und Geschlecht. .
Larsen-Freeman, D., & Anderson, M. (2011). *Techniques and principles in language teaching* (3rd ed.). Oxford University Press.
Lee, C. (2010). An exploratory study of the interlanguage pragmatic comprehension of young learners of English. *Pragmatics, 20*(3), 343–373.
Levey, S. (2017). *Introduction to language development* (2nd ed.). Plural Publishing.
Liddicoat, A. J. (2014). Pragmatics and intercultural mediation in intercultural language learning. *Intercultural Pragmatics, 11*(2), 259–277.
Liddicoat, A. J., & Scarino, A. (2013). *Intercultural language teaching and learning*. Wiley Blackwell.
Ljung, M. (2011). *Swearing: A cross-cultural linguistic study*. Palgrave.
Ludwig, C., & Summer, T. (2023). Approaching taboos and controversial issues in foreign language education. In C. Ludwig & T. Summer (Eds.), *Taboos and controversial issues in foreign language education: Critical language pedagogy in theory, research and practice* (pp. 3–20). Routledge.

Lutzky, U., & Demmen, J. (2013). *Pray* in early modern English drama. *Journal of Historical Pragmatics, 14*(2), 263–284.
Martínez Flor, A., & Usó Juan, E. (2010). Pragmatics and speech act performance. In A. Martínez Flor & E. Usó Juan (Eds.), *Speech act performance: Theoretical, empirical and methodological issues* (pp. 3–22).
McConachy, T. (2022). Pragmatic awareness in intercultural language learning. In I. Kecskes (Ed.), *The Cambridge handbook of intercultural pragmatics* (pp. 766–787). Cambridge University Press.
McConachy, T., & Liddicoat, A. J. (2016). Meta-pragmatic awareness and intercultural competence: The role of reflection and interpretation in intercultural mediation. In F. Dervin & Z. Gross (Eds.), *Intercultural competence in education: Alternative approaches for different times* (pp. 13–30). Palgrave.
McConachy, T., & Liddicoat, A. J. (2022). Introduction: Second language pragmatics for intercultural understanding. In T. McConachy & A. Liddicoat (Eds.), *Teaching and learning second language pragmatics for intercultural understanding* (pp. 1–18). Routledge.
Mitchell, R., Myles, F., & Marsden, E. (2013). *Second language learning theories* (3rd ed.). Routledge.
Morollón Martí, N. (2022). Concept-based instruction for teaching and learning L2 impoliteness. In T. McConachy & A. J. Liddicoat (Eds.), *Teaching and learning second language pragmatics for intercultural understanding* (pp. 126–150). Routledge.
Mugford, G. (2008). How rude! Teaching impoliteness in the second-language classroom. *ELT Journal, 62*(4), 375–384.
Mugford, G. (2019). *Assessing difficult situations in foreign language learning: Confusion, politeness and hostility*. Routledge.
Ninio, A., & Snow, C. (1996). *Pragmatic development*. Westview Press.
Paulston, C. B. (1974). Linguistic and communicative competence. *TESOL Quarterly, 8*(4), 347–362.
Piepho, H. E. (1974). *Kommunikative Kompetenz als übergeordnetes Lernziel im Englischunterricht*. Frankonius Verlag.
Roever, C. (2022). *Teaching and testing second language pragmatics and interaction: A practical guide*. Routledge.
Rose, K. R. (2000). An exploratory cross-sectional study of interlanguage pragmatic development. *Studies in Second Language Acquisition, 22*(1), 27–67.
Savić, M., Economidou-Kogetsidis, M., & Myrset, A. (2021). Young Greek Cypriot and Norwegian EFL learners: Pragmalinguistic development in request production. *Journal of Pragmatics, 180*, 15–34.
Savignon, S. J. (1976). Communicative competence: Theory and classroom practice. In *Keynote address at the central states conference on the teaching of foreign languages*, Detroit, Michigan, April 23, 1976.

Schauer, G. A. (2009). *Interlanguage pragmatic development: The study abroad context.* Continuum/Bloomsbury.
Schauer, G. A. (2016). Assessing intercultural competence. In D. Tsagari & J. Banerjee (Eds.), *Handbook of second language assessment* (pp. 181–202). Mouton de Gruyter.
Schauer, G. A. (2017). "It's really insulting to say something like that to anyone": An investigation of English and German native speakers' impoliteness perceptions. In I. Kecskes & S. Assimakopoulos (Eds.), *Current issues in intercultural pragmatics* (pp. 207–227). John Benjamins.
Schauer, G. A. (2019). *Teaching and learning English in the primary school: Interlanguage pragmatics in the EFL context.* Springer.
Schauer, G. A. (2021). Measuring intercultural competence. In P. Winke & T. Brunfaut (Eds.), *The Routledge handbook of second language acquisition and language testing* (pp. 359–370). Routledge.
Schauer, G. A. (2022). Interlanguage pragmatic development in an instructed secondary school context: Investigating input and output focusing on the speech acts of agreement and disagreement. In N. Halenko & J. Wang (Eds.), *Pragmatics and English language learning* (pp. 143–172). Cambridge University Press.
Schneider, K. P., & Barron, A. (2008). Where pragmatics and dialectology meet: Introducing variational pragmatics. In A. Barron & K. P. Schneider (Eds.), *Variational pragmatics: A focus on regional varieties in pluricentric languages* (pp. 1–34). John Benjamins.
Sercu, L. (2000). *Acquiring intercultural communicative competence from textbooks: The case of Flemish adolescent pupils learning German.* Leuven University Press.
Spencer-Oatey, H. (2010). Intercultural competence and pragmatics research: Examining the interface through studies of intercultural business discourse. In A. Trosborg (Ed.), *Pragmatics across languages and cultures* (pp. 189–216). De Gruyter.
Spencer-Oatey, H., & Franklin, P. (2009). *Intercultural interaction: A multidisciplinary approach to intercultural communication.* Palgrave.
Spitzberg, B. H., & Changnon, G. (2009). Conceptualizing intercultural competence. In D. K. Deardorff (Ed.), *The Sage handbook of intercultural competence* (pp. 2–51). Sage.
Suszczyriska, M. (1999). Apologizing in English, Polish and Hungarian: Different languages, different strategies. *Journal of Pragmatics, 31*(8), 1053–1065.
Taguchi, N. (2017). Interlanguage pragmatics: A historical sketch and future directions. In A. Barron, Y. Gu, & G. Steen (Eds.), *The Routledge handbook of pragmatics* (pp. 153–167). Routledge.
Taguchi, N., & Roever, C. (2017). *Second language pragmatics.* Oxford University Press.

Tatsuki, D. H., & Houck, N. R. (2010). Pragmatics from research to practice: Teaching speech acts. In D. H. Tatsuki & N. R. Houck (Eds.), *Pragmatics: Teaching speech acts* (pp. 1–69). TESOL Press.

Thornbury, S. (2016). Communicative language teaching in theory and practice. In G. Hall (Ed.), *The Routledge handbook of English language teaching* (pp. 224–237). Routledge.

Trosborg, A. (2010). Introduction. In A. Trosborg (Ed.), *Pragmatics across languages and cultures* (pp. 1–39). De Gruyter Mouton.

Van Ek, J. A. (1986). *Objectives for foreign language learning*. Council of Europe.

Warga, M. (2004). *Pragmatische Entwicklung in der Fremdsprache: Der Sprechakt "Aufforderung" im Französischen*. Gunter Narr.

Wilkins, D. (1976). *Notional syllabuses*. Oxford University Press.

Open Access This chapter is licensed under the terms of the Creative Commons Attribution 4.0 International License (http://creativecommons.org/licenses/by/4.0/), which permits use, sharing, adaptation, distribution and reproduction in any medium or format, as long as you give appropriate credit to the original author(s) and the source, provide a link to the Creative Commons licence and indicate if changes were made.

The images or other third party material in this chapter are included in the chapter's Creative Commons licence, unless indicated otherwise in a credit line to the material. If material is not included in the chapter's Creative Commons licence and your intended use is not permitted by statutory regulation or exceeds the permitted use, you will need to obtain permission directly from the copyright holder.

CHAPTER 3

Methodology

3.1 Participants

The questionnaire on which the present study was based was completed by 133 participants, of whom 102 identified as female, 26 as male and one as non-binary.[1] Four participants did not want to share information on their gender identity. Respondents represented a wide range of age groups: 20–29 years old (11 participants), 30–39 years old (32), 40–49 years old (35), 50–59 years old (36), 60+ (17); two participants chose *no comment* here. The percentage distribution of the age groups represented in the sample is provided in Fig. 3.1.

The respondents also had a variety of different native languages: English (53), German (28), Italian (10), Spanish (9), French (8), Portuguese (5), Czech (3), Dutch (3), Japanese (2), Greek (2), Swedish (2), Bahasa Melayu (1), Bahasa Indonesia (1), Catalan (1), Chinese (1), Croatian (1), Persian (1), Russian (1), Turkish (1), Ukrainian (1), Urdu (1) and Yoruba (1).[2]

---

[1] The post-pilot version of the online survey was opened by 219 individuals. Unfortunately, not all of them completed the whole questionnaire, with a considerable number just providing answers to one or two questions. The 133 participants included here provided answers to the majority of the questions.

[2] The numbers add to more than 133 because some of the participants indicated that they had a multilingual upbringing.

© The Author(s) 2024
G. A. Schauer, *Intercultural Competence and Pragmatics*,
https://doi.org/10.1007/978-3-031-44472-2_3

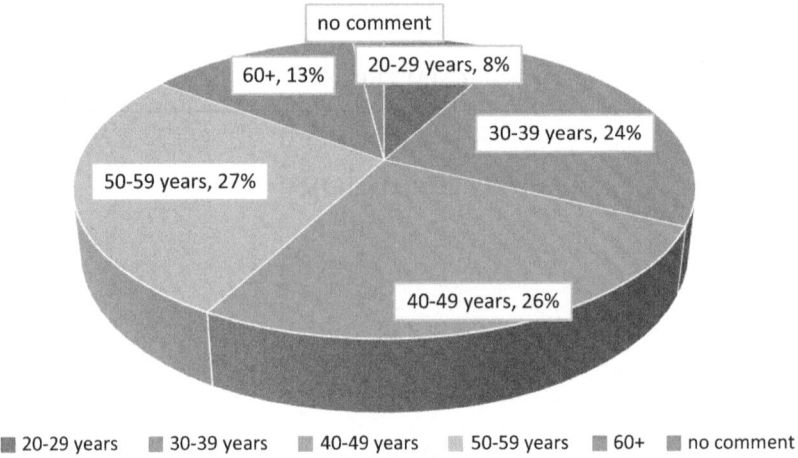

Fig. 3.1 Age groups represented in the sample

The MFL teachers who participated in the study had received their degrees in the following countries: the United Kingdom (52), Germany (29), the United States (16), France (8), Italy (8), Spain (7), Brazil (3), Czech Republic (3), Australia (2), Austria (2), Belgium (2), Canada (2), China (2), Greece (2), Ireland (2), Japan (2), Mexico (2), Portugal(2), Switzerland (2), The Netherlands (2), Turkey (2), Argentina (1), Finland (1), Indonesia (1), Iran (1), Korea (1), Malaysia (1), Moldova (1), New Zealand (1), Nigeria (1), Norway (1), Pakistan (1), Slovakia (1), South Africa (1), Sweden (1) and Ukraine (1).[3]

Seventy-nine of the teachers (59%) stated that they had studied the language(s) they were currently teaching, while 29 (22%) replied that they had studied a modern foreign language but not the one they were currently teaching, and 24 (18%) stated that they had not studied the language(s) they were teaching. One of the respondents chose the no comment option.

Participants in the study represented teachers with different levels of experience, from near novices to highly experienced, with 15 (11%)

---

[3] The total adds to more than 133 because some of the respondents had degrees from more than one country.

3 METHODOLOGY   41

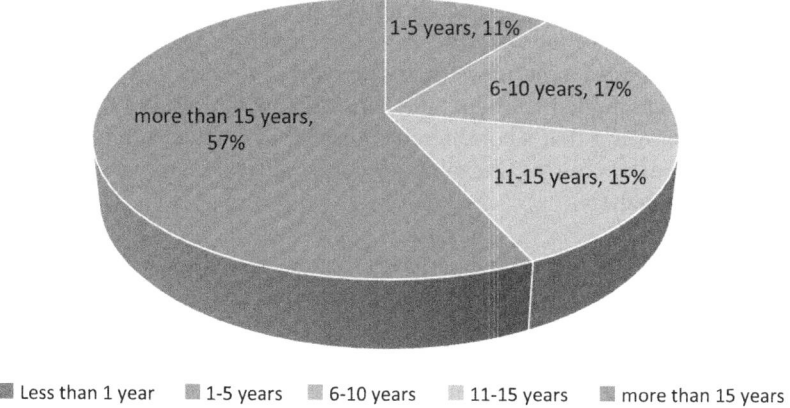

Fig. 3.2 Years of teaching experience of the participants

having taught for 1–5 years, 22 (17%) for 6–10 years, 20 (15%) for 11–15 years and 76 (57%) more than 15 years. This is schematically illustrated in Fig. 3.2.

The respondents were teaching a total of 15 different languages (presented from the highest to the lowest number of teachers teaching a language): English (84), German (24), Italian (13), Spanish (11) French (10), Dutch (4), Swedish (3), Japanese (2), Russian (2), Chinese (1), Czech (1), Korean (1), Norwegian (1), Portuguese (1) and Turkish (1).

The teachers were or had most recently been teaching in the following countries: the United Kingdom (37), Germany (35), France (7), Italy (7), Switzerland (5), Czech Republic (5), Portugal (3), The Netherlands (3), Australia (2), China (2), Greece (2), Japan (2), Austria (1), Canada (1), Croatia (1), Finland (1), Brazil (1), Indonesia (1), Iran (1), Ireland (1), Italy (1), Kazakhstan (1), Malaysia (1), Nigeria (1), Pakistan (1), Spain (1), Turkey (1) and the United States (1).

To find out more about the teaching contexts of the participants, they were asked about the levels (beginner, intermediate, advanced) of the learners that they were teaching. As teachers may work with groups representing different proficiency levels, they could choose more than one level. The teachers' responses showed that 112 (84%) worked with advanced-level, 107 (80%) with intermediate-level and 71 (53%) with beginner-level learners.

The teachers were also asked about the type of course that they teach and were offered a range of different course types to choose from. Since teachers may be teaching more than one type of course, they could again choose all that applied to them, and thus the raw figures add to far more than 133, showing that a considerable number of teachers are involved in different types of courses (meaning, of course, that this not useful grouping for data analysis):

- Pre-sessional courses (i.e., courses that take place prior to the start of the semester/term and prepare students for their studies): 42 participants
- In-sessional courses (i.e., courses that take place during the semester/term): 103 participants
- Intensive courses taught during the regular university semester/term (e.g., courses with a considerable number of hours to increase L2 proficiency in a short period of time): 31 participants
- Intensive courses taught outside the regular university semester/term time (e.g., courses with a considerable number of hours to increase L2 proficiency in a short period of time): 28 participants
- General L2 classes (e.g., classes that are of a more general nature, such as general beginner-level classes): 71 participants
- Academic L2 classes (i.e., classes the focus on specific aspects of L2 academic proficiency, such as essay writing): 87 participants
- Other: 21 participants

The responses by the teachers, illustrated in Fig. 3.3, show that the majority of them teach in-sessional courses (77%), academic L2 courses (65%) and general L2 courses (53%). Pre-sessional or intensive courses (whether offered during or out of semester) are taught by less than a third of the educators. The number of responses to the *other* option illustrates how varied MFL teaching in higher education contexts can be. If they gave this response, there was a free-text field for them to fill in as well, and teachers reported the following: single skills courses (5), English for Specific Purposes (5), business language (4), intercultural communication or culture (3), translation or mediation (2), area studies or country studies (2), English for university staff (2), foundation course (1), English for refugees[4] (1) and language test preparation (1).

---

[4] Unfortunately, no further information was provided. It could be the case that this refers to special language courses offered by individual higher education institutions that are specifically targeted at students who had to flee their home countries.

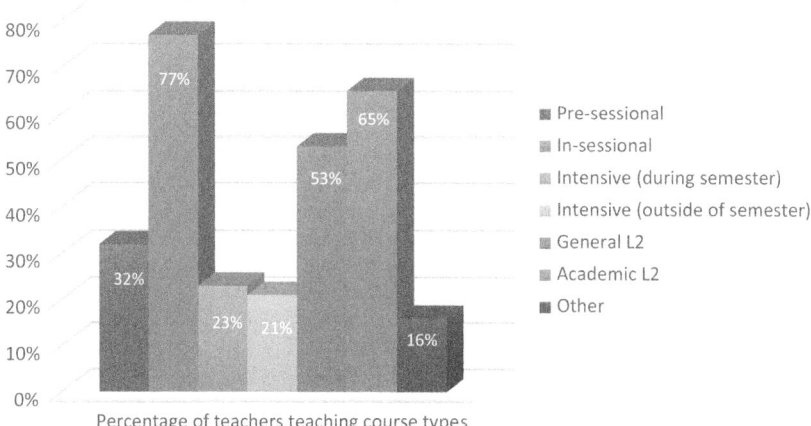

Fig. 3.3 Course types taught by the respondents

In my discussion of the findings in Chaps. 4, 5, 6, 7 and 8, I focus on the whole group—that is, all 133 MFL teachers—as well as on individual groups of teachers who were either only teaching one language or who indicated in the survey that they were thinking of a particular language when taking part in the study.[5] However, analysis of individual groups has only been done when there were at least three teachers in the sample who were teaching that language. There are only seven languages that are represented in this way, covering a total of 115 teachers in the sample (86%). Some background information on each language group is included in Table 3.1; with regard to other personal background factors such as years of teaching experience and age distribution, the individual language groups tended to resemble the sample as a whole.

---

[5] Twenty-nine of the teachers indicated that they were teaching more than one modern foreign language. However, if these teachers indicated in question 10e of the survey that they had focused on a particular language they were teaching while they were completing the questionnaire, their responses have been analysed as though they were only teaching that language in all the analyses that focus on the responses of teachers teaching one of the seven languages represented by more than three teachers (English, German, Italian, Spanish, French, Dutch and Swedish).

Table 3.1 Overview of the groups of teachers who taught each of the languages represented by more than three teachers

Language	Number of teachers	F/M/NB/NC	Native language(s) of the teachers
English	75	56/18/0/1	English (45), German (8), Italian (4), Czech (3), French (2), Greek (2), Portuguese (2), Bahasa Indonesia (1), Bahasa Melayu (1), Croatian (1), Japanese (1), Persian (1), Russian (1), Spanish (1), Turkish (1), Ukrainian (1), Urdu (1), Yoruba (1)
German	11	10/0/1/0	German (10), English (1)
Italian	10	8/2/0/0	Italian (4), English (3), Portuguese (2), German (1)
Spanish	7	7/0/0/0	Spanish (7), Catalan (1)
French	6	2/4/0/0	French (5), English (1)
Dutch	3	2/0/0/1	Dutch (3)
Swedish	3	3/0/0/0	Swedish (2), German (1)

Note: As mentioned, some teachers provided more than one native language (e.g., there was a Spanish/Catalan bilingual). Since all first languages mentioned by group members are listed, the total number of first languages sometimes exceeds the number of teachers in the group; *F* Female, *M* Male, *NB* Non-binary, *NC* No comment

3.2 Instrument

The data for this study were elicited with an online survey (via https://www.umfrageonline.com) directed at teachers of any modern language taught as an L2 in a higher education context (e.g., language centres). The complete questionnaire consisting of 18 questions (some of which have several parts) can be found in the Appendix to this chapter. Questions 1–9 address different aspects of intercultural and pragmatic competence either with regard to teachers' views, teaching realities or the teachers' educational background. Questions 10–17 are personal (background) questions. Question 18 gave teachers the opportunity to comment on any issue they wished relevant to the survey (since the comments tended to contain questions about further studies and other personal messages, they are not discussed in this book). Teachers' responses to questions 10–17 have been presented in Sect. 3.1. Their answers to the research questions will be analysed and discussed as follows: questions 2 and 3 in Chap. 4; questions 1, 4, 5 and 6 in Chap. 5; question 7 in Chap. 6; question 8 in Chap. 7; and question 9 in Chap. 8.

3.3 Procedure

The development of the online survey began in 2021. The design of the survey and the development of the individual questions was influenced by a previous online survey that was conducted in 2020 and was directed at English as a foreign language (EFL) teachers working with different learner groups (primary, secondary and tertiary/adult). The first results of this earlier study were published in Schauer (2022).

The present survey grew out of my reflections on the earlier survey as well as discussions with other researchers on that initial publication; as I have stated in the acknowledgements, I am particularly grateful to Troy McConachy for his comments on my earlier study, without which this one would not exist.

The survey used to collect data for this monograph was devised in April and May 2021. Two of the research questions included in the present survey (questions 2 and 4) were similar to questions included in the earlier online survey directed at EFL teachers; the remaining questions were specifically developed for this questionnaire. The questionnaire was piloted in early May 2021 with two participants who subsequently did not take part in the actual study. I also completed the questionnaire myself to check for any issues that needed clarification. Some minor modifications were made based on the pilot participants' suggestions and the survey was then made available to teachers in late May.

I posted about the study on my social media sites, inviting teachers of modern foreign languages working in higher education to take part; these posts were kindly reposted by other scholars and institutions. In addition, I also emailed researchers, associations, research groups and institutions with the link and asked them to make potential participants aware of the study. MFL teachers then took part by clicking on the link provided and completing the questionnaire. The survey was available for participation from the end of May 2021 to the beginning of August 2021.

This concludes the methodology chapter. The results of questions 1 to 9 are presented in Chaps. 4, 5, 6, 7 and 8.

Appendix: Survey Questions

The questions included in the online survey are presented below. The questions are in the original order. Minor changes have been made to correct typos.

Question 1. How important is it for you to teach the following skills and competences in L2 language teaching?

- Academic listening skills in the L2 (e.g., listening to lectures)
- Academic reading skills in the L2 (e.g., coping with unknown words)
- Academic speaking skills (e.g., how to address university staff)
- Academic writing skills (e.g., how to write an essay in the L2)
- Academic discussion skills (e.g., preference for direct versus indirect discussion style in the L2)
- General language skills (e.g., listening, reading, speaking, writing) in non-academic contexts
- L2 expressions that can be used to react in an appropriate and sympathetic manner when encountering cultural differences

Mediation skills

- Strategies that equip the learner with practical skills for handling intercultural encounters

Answer options for each skill/competence: Very unimportant; unimportant; neither important nor unimportant; important; very important; don't know.

Question 2. Which terms do you associate with intercultural competence in the L2? Please select all that that apply.

- Ability to produce situationally appropriate language
- Ability to recognize conflicts and deal with conflicts
- Adaptability
- Awareness of different ways of thinking, orientations and values
- Being able to mediate and help individuals who do not speak the target language
- Being understanding and sympathetic when encountering cultural differences
- Correct pronunciation
- Curiosity
- Efficiency
- Empathy
- Flexibility
- Grammatical competence
- Knowledge of celebrations, geography and history in countries in which the L2 is the official language
- Knowledge of gender-neutral language forms (e.g., *they* instead of *she* or *he* in English, *Politiker*innen* in German)
- Knowledge of political structures and systems in the countries in which the L2 is the official language
- Knowledge of politeness norms
- Knowledge of vocabulary items that have appeared in recent years (e.g., *Brexit* in English, *AHA-Regel* in German)
- Mindfulness
- Motivation
- Openness
- Patience
- Self-reflection
- Strategies that equip the learner with practical skills for handling intercultural encounters
- Tolerance
- None
- Don't know

(continued)

(continued)

Question 3. Are the following linguistic aspects part of intercultural competence in your view?

- Acronyms & abbreviations
- Conversational openings and closings (e.g., greetings, "how are you" questions)
- Expressing negative emotions (e.g., sadness, anger)
- Expressing positive emotions (e.g., happiness)
- False friends
- How to agree and disagree in the L2
- How to apologize in different situations
- How to ask for something (e.g., extension, goods, favours)
- How to complain about someone or something
- Impolite & aggressive expressions
- Swear words & taboo language
- Vocabulary

Answer options for each linguistic aspect: Yes; no; don't know

Question 4. How important is it for you to teach the following facts/information about the countries and cultures in which the L2 is an official language or native language?[6]

- Biology & ecology
- Celebrations
- Different ways of thinking, orientations and values
- Economy & finance
- Geography
- Healthcare and medicine
- History
- Infrastructure and travel (e.g., airports)
- International relations
- Literature, art & music
- Political systems & structures
- Wars & conflicts (e.g., the Vietnam War, The Troubles)
- Important national symbols & flags
- Legal system
- Religious communities & religious symbols, holidays, etc.
- Well-known individuals of the target country (e.g., artists, politicians, scientists, sportspeople)

Answer options for each area: Very unimportant; unimportant; neither important nor unimportant; important; very important; don't know.

(*continued*)

---

[6] Terms that are included as options in this question were based on intercultural competence definitions or frameworks (Byram, 1997, 2009; Fantini, 1995, 2019; Liddicoat & Scarino, 2013; Ting-Toomey & Dorjee, 2015) and publications by the Standing Conference of the Ministers of Education and Cultural Affairs in Germany (KMK, 1996/2013, 2003, 2004), as well as including my own additions. A similar question was included in the survey used for Schauer (2022).

(continued)

Question 5. How important is it for you to include the following in your language classes?

- Materials focusing on culture shock
- Materials focusing on different age groups (e.g., young adults, pensioners)
- Materials written by individuals from different countries
- Equal representation of texts focusing on males and females
- Newspaper articles originating from newspapers that differ with regard to their political views
- Texts addressing the experiences and views of individuals with different religious beliefs (e.g., Catholics and Protestants in Northern Ireland)
- Texts addressing the experience of immigrants
- Texts addressing the experience of individuals with disabilities
- Texts addressing LGBTIQ issues
- Texts addressing study abroad experiences
- Texts representing the views/experience of individuals with different ethnic backgrounds

Answer options for each item: Very unimportant; unimportant; neither important nor unimportant; important; very important; don't know.

Question 6. How important is it for you to teach the following language aspects when teaching a foreign language?

- Acronyms & abbreviations
- Conversational openings and closings (e.g., greetings, "how are you" questions)
- Correct pronunciation
- Expressing negative emotions (e.g., sadness, anger)
- Expressing positive emotions (e.g., happiness)
- False friends
- Grammar (e.g., tenses, syntax)
- How to agree and disagree in the L2
- How to apologize in different situations
- How to ask for something (e.g., extension, goods, favours)
- How to complain about someone or something
- Impolite & aggressive expressions
- Language that is appropriate to the situation
- Swear words & taboo language
- Vocabulary that is used in everyday life
- Vocabulary that may be mainly used in academic contexts
- Vocabulary that is used in specific professions (e.g., medical terms)
- Vocabulary that may no longer be in use (e.g., *pray* meaning "please")
- Vocabulary that may only be used in a particular region or country in which the L2 is the official language (e.g., the German "*Grüß Gott*" [lit. Greet God] in southern Germany and Austria)

Answer options for each aspect: Very unimportant; unimportant; neither important nor unimportant; important; very important; don't know.

Question 7a. Are you familiar with pragmatic competence?

- Yes
- No
- Don't know

(continued)

Question 7b. For the purposes of this questionnaire, pragmatic competence in an L2 will be defined as a person's ability to communicate effectively and appropriately in a second or foreign language (L2) and to comprehend the L2 even if indirect or conventional expressions are used. How are intercultural competence and pragmatic competence connected in your view?

- They are different concepts that are not connected
- Pragmatic competence is part of intercultural competence
- Don't know
- Other connection, namely [space for individual answer]

Question 8a. Do gender-neutral expressions or pronouns exist in the L2 you are teaching? If your answer is *no*, *don't know* or *no comment* please then proceed to question 9.

- Yes
- No
- Don't know
- No comment
- Other [space for individual answer]

Question 8b. If gender-neutral language options exist in your L2, do you teach them? If your answer is *yes*, please proceed to question 8c. If your answer is *no*, please proceed to question 8d. If your answer is *no comment* please proceed to question 9.

- Yes
- No
- No comment
- Other [space for individual answer]

Question 8c. If you are teaching gender-neutral language options, you can share your reasons for doing so here. Please then proceed to question 9.

Question 8d. If you are not teaching gender-neutral forms, you can share your reasons for not doing so here.

Question 9a. Was intercultural competence addressed during your university studies?

- Yes
- No
- Don't know
- No comment

Question 9b. Do you associate particular scholars with intercultural competence? If so, please select or add the name(s) below. If not, please move on to the next question.

- Byram
- Fantini
- Savignon
- Spencer-Oatey
- Ting-Toomey
- [Space for individual answer]

(continued)

(continued)

Question 10a. Which L2(s) do you teach?[7]

- English
- French
- Spanish
- German
- Italian
- Arabic
- Chinese
- Japanese
- Russian
- Another language, namely [space for individual answer]

Question 10b. Which L2 levels do you teach? Please tick all that apply.

- Beginner
- Intermediate
- Advanced

Question 10c. What kind of courses do you teach? Please tick all that apply.

- Pre-sessional courses (i.e. courses that take place prior to the start of the semester/term and prepare students for their studies)
- In-sessional courses (i.e. courses that take place during the semester/term time)
- Intensive courses during the semester/term (e.g., courses with a considerable number of hours to increase L2 proficiency in a short period of time)
- Intensive courses out of semester/term time (e.g., courses with a considerable number of hours to increase L2 proficiency in a short period of time)
- General L2 classes (e.g., classes that are of a more general nature, such as general beginner level classes)
- Academic L2 classes (i.e., classes the focus on specific aspects of L2 academic proficiency, such as essay writing)
- Other [space for individual answer]

Question 10d. Do you teach more than one L2? If not, please move on to question 11.

- Yes
- No

Question 10e. If you teach more than one L2, was there a specific L2 that you primarily thought of when completing the questionnaire?

- No
- Don't know
- No comment
- Yes, namely [space for individual answer]

(continued)

---

[7] The questions about personal background in questions 10a, 10b, 10d, 11, 15, 16 and 17 were based on similar questions in Sercu et al. (2005).

(continued)

Question 11. How long have you been teaching the L2(s)?
- Less than 1 year
- 1–5 years
- 6–10 years
- 11–15 years
- More than 15 years
- No comment

Question 12. Did you study the L2(s) you are currently teaching at a higher education institution? • Yes • No • No, but I studied another modern foreign language (e.g., French) • No comment

Question 13. In which country or countries did you receive your degree(s)?[Space for individual answer]

Question 14. In which country are you currently teaching or have been teaching most recently if you are retired or currently not teaching?[Space for individual answer]

Question 15. You are • Female • Male • Non-binary • No comment • Other, namely [space for individual answer]

Question 16. Your native language is/Your native languages are[Space for individual answer]

Question 17. Your age group is • 20–29 years • 30–39 years • 40–49 years • 50–59 years • 60+ • No comment

Question 18. If you have any comments on issues that you encountered in this questionnaire, you can share them here.[Space for individual answer]

REFERENCES

Byram, M. (1997). *Teaching and assessing intercultural communicative competence.* Multilingual Matters.

Byram, M. (2009). Intercultural speaker and the pedagogy of foreign language education. In D. Deardorff (Ed.), *The SAGE handbook of intercultural competence* (pp. 321–332). Sage.

Fantini, A. E. (1995). Introduction-language, culture and world view: Exploring the nexus. *International Journal of Intercultural Relations, 19*(2), 143–153.

Fantini, A. E. (2019). *Intercultural communicative competence in educational exchange: A multinational perspective.* Routledge.

KMK. (1996/2013). *Interkulturelle Bildung und Erziehung in der Schule.* https://www.kmk.org/fileadmin/veroeffentlichungen_beschluesse/1996/1996_10_25-Interkulturelle-Bildung.pdf

KMK. (2003). *Beschlüsse der Kultusministerkonferenz: Bildungsstandards für die erste Fremdsprache (Englisch/Französisch) für den mittleren Schulabschluss (Jahrgangsstufe 10).* https://www.kmk.org/fileadmin/veroeffentlichungen_beschluesse/2003/2003_12_04-BS-erste-Fremdsprache.pdf

KMK. (2004). *Beschlüsse der Kultusministerkonferenz: Bildungsstandards für die erste Fremdsprache (Englisch/Französisch) für den Hauptschulabschluss (Jahrgangsstufe 9)*. https://www.kmk.org/fileadmin/veroeffentlichungen_beschluesse/2004/2004_10_15-Bildungsstandards-ersteFS-Haupt.pdf

Liddicoat, A. J., & Scarino, A. (2013). *Intercultural language teaching and learning*. Wiley Blackwell.

Schauer, G. A. (2022). Intercultural competence and pragmatics in the L2 classroom: Views of in-service EFL teachers in primary, secondary and adult education. In A. J. Liddicoat & T. McConachy (Eds.), *Teaching and learning L2 pragmatics for intercultural understanding* (pp. 173–191). Routledge.

Sercu, L., Bandura, E., Castro, P., Davcheva, L., Laskaridou, C., Lundgren, U., García, M., del C., M., & Ryan, P. (2005). *Foreign language teachers and intercultural competence: An international investigation*. Multilingual Matters.

Ting-Toomey, S., & Dorjee, T. (2015). Intercultural and intergroup communication competence: Toward an integrative perspective. In A. F. Hannawa & B. H. Spitzberg (Eds.), *Communication competence* (pp. 503–538). De Gruyter Mouton.

Open Access This chapter is licensed under the terms of the Creative Commons Attribution 4.0 International License (http://creativecommons.org/licenses/by/4.0/), which permits use, sharing, adaptation, distribution and reproduction in any medium or format, as long as you give appropriate credit to the original author(s) and the source, provide a link to the Creative Commons licence and indicate if changes were made.

The images or other third party material in this chapter are included in the chapter's Creative Commons licence, unless indicated otherwise in a credit line to the material. If material is not included in the chapter's Creative Commons licence and your intended use is not permitted by statutory regulation or exceeds the permitted use, you will need to obtain permission directly from the copyright holder.

CHAPTER 4

Results: Components of Intercultural Competence

4.1 OVERVIEW OF TERMS ASSOCIATED WITH INTERCULTURAL COMPETENCE IN THE L2

As discussed in Chap. 2, there are many different definitions, conceptualizations and frameworks of intercultural competence. Apart from being discussed in the academic literature on intercultural competence (e.g., Byram, 1997; Deardorff, 2006; Fantini, 2019), intercultural competence is frequently referred to in MFL curricula (e.g., KMK, 1996/2013, in Germany; Department of Education and Skills, 2017, in Ireland; Ministry of Education, 2016, in Ontario, Canada) and in government publications on language standards (e.g., KMK, 2003, 2012), as well as in publications by international institutions (e.g.,CoE, 2008, 2014; UNESCO, 2013). In addition, teachers develop their own conceptualizations of intercultural competence based on their own experiences. In order to obtain insights into the role of pragmatics in the conceptualizations of intercultural competence held by the sample of teachers represented in this research project, it is important to first examine how they conceptualize IC.

For this reason, this chapter starts by considering the teachers' responses to question 2 in the survey, a general question about the components of intercultural competence that not only offers linguistic and pragmatic options but follows a broader approach to include other elements featured in existing IC frameworks. The items included were based on Byram (1997, 2009), Fantini (1995, 2019), Liddicoat and Scarino (2013), Ting-Toomey and Dorjee (2015) and publications by the Standing Conference

© The Author(s) 2024
G. A. Schauer, *Intercultural Competence and Pragmatics*,
https://doi.org/10.1007/978-3-031-44472-2_4

of the Ministers of Education and Cultural Affairs in Germany (KMK, 1996/2013, 2003, 2004), as well as including a number of additions of my own.

Figure 4.1 reports on the results of the responses to question 2 and presents the terms that the 133 teachers in this study associated with intercultural competence. The teachers were invited to select as many of the terms as they wished that they considered to be part of intercultural competence. The results are presented according to teachers' choices (i.e., beginning with the component chosen by the largest number of teachers cascading down to the term chosen by the fewest educators), rather than in their original order in the survey (see the Appendix in Chap. 3 for the original sequence).

The results show that all items suggested as possible components of intercultural competence were selected by at least some teachers. *Efficiency* was the component chosen by the fewest teachers (13 teachers, representing 10% of participants), while *awareness of different ways of thinking, orientations and values* was selected by the highest number (122 teachers, 92%). The items in the second and third places were *being understanding and sympathetic when encountering cultural differences* (87%) and *knowledge of politeness norms* (84%).

The top three items are interesting because two of them were also chosen by large number of participants in a study that I conducted with English L2 teachers in primary, secondary and adult education that featured a similar question (Schauer, 2022). In that study, the top three items chosen by the 64 educators were *being understanding and sympathetic when encountering cultural differences* (94%), *openness* (88%) and *knowledge of politeness norms in the target language* (86%). The item in the 2022 study that was equivalent to the top-ranked item in the present study—*knowledge of different ways of thinking, orientations and values*—was chosen by 83% of the EFL teachers, thus putting it in the fourth place out of 22 items. Interestingly, however, only 74% of the teachers in adult education chose this item compared to 100% of the secondary school teachers and 80% of the primary school educators. A possible explanation for the popularity of this item in the present study could be the slight change in the wording from *knowledge* (2022) to *awareness* (present study). Other reasons could include the slightly different participant groups, such as having only teachers of English in 2022, but teachers of a range of modern languages in the present study. As the results of the analysis of question 2 according to languages will show (see Table 4.1), while the top-ranked

4 RESULTS: COMPONENTS OF INTERCULTURAL COMPETENCE   55

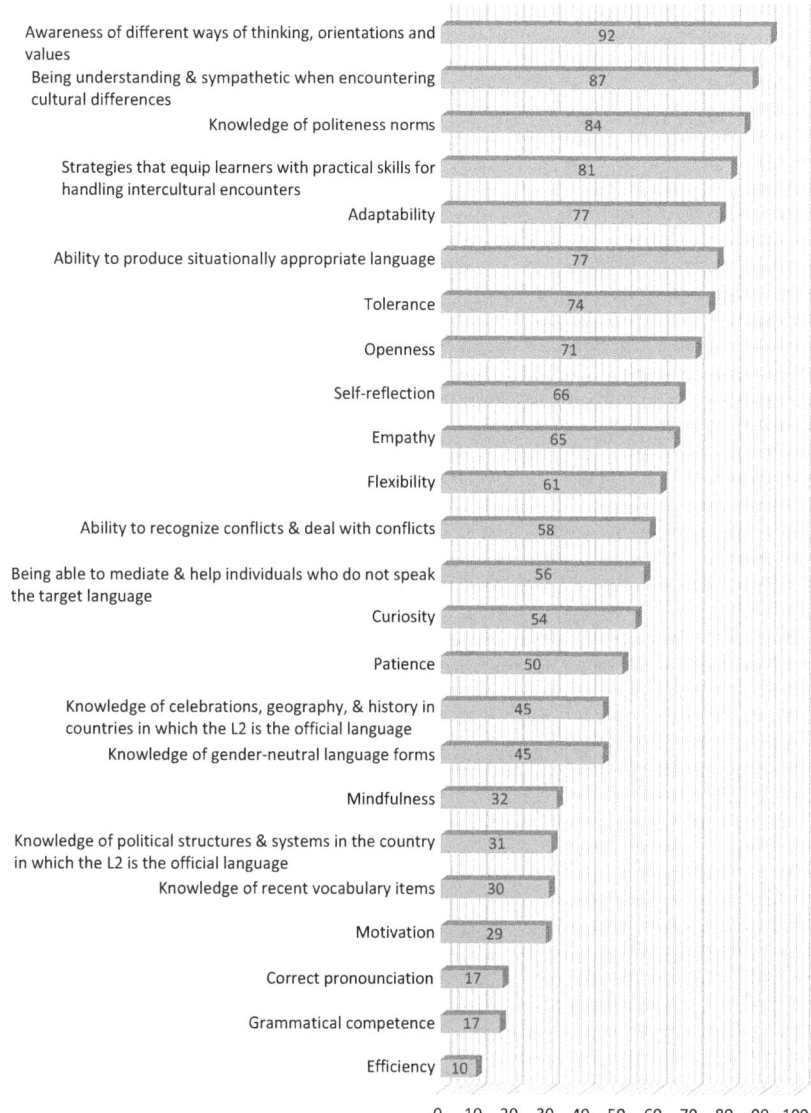

Fig. 4.1 Percentage of teachers who marked each potential component as being associated with L2 intercultural competence

Table 4.1 Percentage of teachers in each language group who selected each potential component as being associated with intercultural competence

	Language group							
	E	G	I	Sp	F	D	Sw	Total
Awareness of different ways of thinking, orientations and values	91	82	100	100	100	100	67	92
Being understanding and sympathetic when encountering cultural differences	85	82	100	100	67	100	67	87
Knowledge of politeness norms	84	73	100	57	100	67	67	84
Strategies that equip the learner with practical skills for handling intercultural encounters	81	73	100	86	83	67	67	81
Adaptability	81	73	90	71	83	0.0	67	77
Ability to produce situationally appropriate language	76	73	100	71	83	100	67	77
Tolerance	73	73	100	86	83	33	67	74
Openness	69	64	90	43	83	67	67	71
Self-reflection	63	82	90	43	67	67	33	66
Empathy	68	46	80	57	50	33	33	65
Flexibility	63	64	40	43	50	33	67	61
Ability to recognize conflicts and deal with conflicts	60	55	50	43	50	67	67	58
Being able to mediate and help individuals who do not speak the target language	49	55	70	86	67	33	67	56
Curiosity	51	18	70	57	67	67	100	54
Patience	51	55	60	14	50	33	67	50
Knowledge of celebrations, geography and history in countries in which the L2 is the official language	33	46	90	43	50	33	67	45
Knowledge of gender-neutral language forms (e.g., *they* instead of *she* or *he* in English, *Politiker*innen* in German)	52	64	50	29	33	0	0	45
Mindfulness	29	46	30	29	33	0	67	32
Knowledge of political structures and systems in the countries in which the L2 is the official language	24	36	50	14	50	67	33	31
Knowledge of vocabulary items that appeared in recent years (e.g., *Brexit* in English, *AHA-Regel* in German)	35	9	30	29	50	0	33	30
Motivation	32	9	20	14	33	0	100	29
Correct pronunciation	21	0	20	0	0	0	33	17
Grammatical competence	19	0	30	0	17	0	0	17

(*continued*)

Table 4.1 (continued)

	Language group							
	E	G	I	Sp	F	D	Sw	Total
Efficiency	12	9	0	0	0	0	0	10

Note: Total score represents all teachers of all languages, and so corresponds to the data presented in Fig. 4.1

Key to languages: *E* English, *G* German, *I* Italian, *Sp* Spanish, *F* French, *D* Dutch, *Sw* Swedish

item in this study was chosen by 100% of some MFL teacher groups (e.g., those focusing on Dutch, French, Italian and Spanish), it was only selected by 91% of the English teachers in this study.

In addition to the second-ranked item, *being understanding and sympathetic when encountering cultural differences* (87%), components related to attitudes and characteristics were chosen by a large number of the teachers, which supports their inclusion in IC frameworks (e.g., Byram, 1997; Deardorff, 2006; Fantini, 2019). The following were selected by at least half of the teachers: *adaptability* (77%), *tolerance* (74%), *openness* (71%), *self-reflection* (66%), *empathy* (65%), *flexibility* (61%), *curiosity* (54%) and *patience* (50%). All of these components were also chosen by more than half of the teachers in the 2022 study, thus indicating that they are likely to be considered to be IC components by a large number of MFL teachers.

Regarding the language-related items, the findings reveal that those that are very clearly related to pragmatic concerns rank highly. As mentioned above, *knowledge of politeness norms* is in third place with 84% and *ability to produce situationally appropriate language* is in sixth place with 77%. Both items were also frequently selected by the English teachers in the 2022 study (86% chose *politeness*, while 80% chose *appropriate language*). This indicates that core pragmatic concerns—that is, situationally appropriate and polite language—are widely considered to be components of intercultural competence by MFL teachers.

Apart from the items that are of a more overt pragmatic nature, those that are perhaps more covert—*ability to recognize conflicts and deal with conflicts* and *knowledge of gender-neutral language forms*—were chosen by 58% and 45% of the teachers in the study, respectively. While the item about gender was not included in the 2022 study, that about *conflict* was chosen by 64% of the English L2 teachers in the 2022 paper. This gives further support to the inclusion of pragmatic aspects as essential components of IC frameworks. It also highlights that diversity aspects such as gender-neutral language ought to receive more attention in IC research and discussions.

Compared to other linguistic items, such as *knowledge of recent vocabulary items* (30%), *correct pronunciation* (17%) and *grammatical competence* (17%), *strategies that equip learners with practical skills for handling intercultural encounters*, an item that can also refer to language skills, was rated highly (81%). This mirrors the findings from the 2022 study, in which grammar and pronunciation were also chosen by a smaller number of teachers, 16 and 11%, respectively (vocabulary was not included as a possible component), while *strategies that equip the learner with practical skills for handling intercultural encounters in the foreign language* was also chosen by a considerable number of teachers (70%) in that study. This suggests that structural linguistic elements tend to be less frequently regarded as components of IC, while strategies for handling intercultural encounters (potentially including linguistic ones) are.

Interestingly, the knowledge items that are often addressed in teaching materials—*knowledge of celebrations, geography and history* and *knowledge of political structures and systems*—were chosen by less than 50% of the teachers (45% and 31%, respectively). While *knowledge of political structures and systems* was also chosen by less than 50% of the teachers in the 2022 study (45%), *knowledge of celebrations, geography and history* was considered to be a component of IC by 64% of the English L2 teachers in that study. Although it could be assumed that this high score may solely relate to the primary and secondary school teachers in the 2022 study—and it is true that 100% of the primary school teachers in the 2022 considered this item to be an IC component—it should be noted that 64% of the teachers in adult education in that survey thought likewise. A possible explanation for the different results could then be sought in the MFL taught, but as Table 4.1 will show, the English teachers in the present study were a teacher group that had one of the lowest scores for this item compared to some of the others, which suggests that this explanation may not be promising in this case either.

However, similarities and differences in teachers' views on IC components based on the language they are teaching are nevertheless worth exploring, since they can provide insights into how homogenous or heterogenous the views of modern foreign language teachers in the study are.

Table 4.1 provides an overview of the intercultural component scores according to the language the teachers focused on when completing the questionnaire. In the questionnaire, the respondents were asked which languages they were teaching and, if they were teaching more than one language, which MFL they were thinking of when completing the questionnaire (see Sect. 3.1). Table 4.1 includes the data of those teachers that were either teaching a single language or that provided information on which language they were thinking of when completing the questionnaire (where there were at least three teachers of that language): 75 English teachers, 11 German teachers, 10 Italian teachers, seven Spanish teachers, six French teachers, three Dutch teachers and three Swedish teachers. Due to the difference in group sizes and the extremely small number of participants in two of the groups, no statistical analyses were conducted.

Prior to discussing the results, it is important to re-state that the number of teachers representing each individual group varies considerably, with the English teachers in the clear majority and a higher representation of teachers of Germanic languages (English, German, Dutch and Swedish) than Romance languages (Italian, Spanish and French): the data of the 115 teachers discussed here was provided by 92 Germanic language teachers and 23 Romance language teachers. Thus, as is the case in the analyses and discussions that focus solely on the whole group data, it needs to be borne in mind that English in particular and Germanic languages as a whole are represented by a larger number of teachers than the other languages.[1]

The first notable observation is that there is no single item that was chosen by 90% of all groups. Even though the highest-ranked whole group item with 92%, *awareness of different ways of thinking, orientations and values*, was chosen by 100% of the Italian, Spanish, French and Dutch teachers, it was selected by 91% of the English, 82% of the German and only 67% of the Swedish teachers. This item could suggest that teachers of the three Romance languages might evaluate some components in similar ways, but while the Italian and French percentages are the same in some instances (e.g., 100% for *knowledge of politeness norms*, compared to 57%

---

[1] Since the number of teachers focusing on Germanic and Romance languages is so uneven, it was not considered that contrasting the teachers' choices and views based on language families would offer any additional insights. Instead, a more fine-grained analysis focusing on the actual languages taught was conducted.

of the Spanish teachers) and similar in others (e.g., 90 and 80%, respectively, for *openness* compared to 43% of the Spanish teachers), there are also instances where the percentage scores of one Romance teacher group is closer to one of the Germanic teacher groups.

For example, *knowledge of gender-neutral language forms* was considered to be an IC component by 52% of the English teachers, 64% of the German teachers and 50% of the Italian teachers, but only by 33% of the French teachers and 29% of the Spanish teachers. The differences in the perception of diversity aspects with regard to the representation of gender may be due to different societal and political developments of the past 40 years that resulted in a broader acceptance of gender-neutral language in the English-speaking countries (e.g., American Psychological Association, 2020) than appears to be the case in Romance countries (e.g., Erdocia, 2022; Formato, 2018) or in Germany, where although gender-neutral forms were introduced years ago, (far-)right parties are now attempting to prohibit their use. Gender-neutral language will be discussed in more detail in Chap. 7.

When it comes to educators teaching the Germanic languages English and German, the results reveal that these two groups are often similar with regard to the percentage of teachers that selected potential IC components: for example, *being understanding and sympathetic when encountering cultural differences* was chosen by 85% of the English and by 82% of the German teachers, and *patience* was chosen by 51 of the English and by 55% of the German teachers. However, there are also items where the percentage scores of the two groups differed considerably; for example, *self-reflection* was chosen by 63% of the English but by 82% of the German teachers, while *knowledge of vocabulary items that appeared in recent years* was selected by 35 of the English yet only by 9% of the German teachers. Due to the small number of participants in the Dutch and Swedish teacher groups (three teachers each) not much can be said about them, but it is notable that there are eight potential IC items not chosen by any member of the Dutch group (including *adaptability, mindfulness* and *grammatical competence*), while there were only three items which none of the Swedish group selected *(knowledge of gender-neutral language forms, grammatical competence* and *efficiency)*.

Of the two items that are most clearly related to pragmatic competence, *ability to produce situationally appropriate language* and *knowledge of politeness norms*, the language group percentages ranged from 100 (Italian,

Dutch) to 67 (Swedish) for the former, and from 100 (Italian, French) to 57 (Spanish), thus always clearly remaining above half of the teachers in each group.

Overall, the results of the analysis of language-based IC components shows that analysing teachers' views according to the language they are focusing on can provide additional insights that may not be offered by a combined overview analysis reporting on the data of teachers teaching different modern foreign languages. Further studies are needed in this field to shed more light on the connections between the language taught and teachers' views of intercultural competence components, in particular ones that involve a higher number of modern foreign languages teachers not focused on English and that ideally also have a higher number of teachers in each individual language group included in the study.

The discussion has so far centred on an overview of the IC components representing a wide variety of abilities, attitudes and characteristics, knowledge, and skills. In the following section, I will focus on specific aspects of linguistic IC components that were included in the study to obtain a better understanding of the role of pragmatics in IC.

4.2 Linguistic Components of Intercultural Competence

As stated in Chap. 2, although the link between communicative competence, intercultural competence and pragmatics seems very obvious, since "effective and appropriate language use" is a recurring theme in all three fields, the relationship between pragmatics and IC has rarely been explicitly addressed in well-known frameworks (see also Jackson, 2019; McConachy & Liddicoat, 2022; Schauer, 2022). To explore teachers' views of the link between core pragmatic components, speech acts and (im)politeness, the third question in the survey, *Are the following linguistic aspects part of intercultural competence in your view?*, focused largely on pragmatic components, but without including the terms pragmatics or speech acts, as previous research has shown that L2 teachers may not be familiar with these terms (Savvidou & Economidou-Kogetsidis, 2019). This third question featured 12 items, of which five closely correspond to speech acts, listed below with the actual wording of the item in questionnaire followed by terminology used in pragmatics research:

1. Conversational openings and closings (e.g., greetings, how are you questions)—which are either referred to as openings and closings in the pragmatics literature or may be referred to as greetings and leave-takings.
2. How to agree and disagree in the L2—agreements and disagreements,
3. How to apologize in different situations—apologies.
4. How to ask for something (e.g., extension, goods, favours)—requests.
5. How to complain about someone or something—complaints.

In addition to the five speech acts, I also included two items that focused on emotions, worded as *expressing positive emotions* (e.g., *happiness*) and *expressing negative emotions* (e.g., *sadness, anger*). While the latter is more overtly linked to the two impoliteness items that I have included—*impolite & aggressive expressions* and *swear words & taboo language*—the former could also be regarded to be a pragmatic item based on its interpretation by the individual teacher (see, e.g., Dewaele, 2015, 2016; Potts & Schwarz, 2008; Rintell, 1984). For example, if expressing positive emotions is considered to refer to complimenting or congratulating someone else, it would firmly place it in the field of pragmatics, as both are speech acts. If, however, the two items are interpreted to solely refer to knowledge of vocabulary, then teachers may not have linked them to pragmatics. Likewise, the second impoliteness item, *swear words & taboo language*, could also be considered to purely refer to vocabulary knowledge if the impact of the use of such language on other interlocutors is disregarded or if teachers were thinking of instances where a swear word might be used by someone who is alone (e.g., as a result of dropping a cup of tea). Two of the remaining three items in this question are more firmly based in the field of lexis, *vocabulary* and *acronyms and abbreviations*, whereas the third, *false friends*,[2] could refer to a wide range of linguistic phenomena but is most likely to also be thought of as related to vocabulary.

Figure 4.2 presents the results of the whole group, indicating the percentage of the 133 teachers who chose *yes*, *no* and *don't know* to the question of whether each linguistic aspect formed part of intercultural competence. The results show that the five speech acts are considered to be IC components by the vast majority of the teachers: conversational

---

[2] See footnotes 8 and 9 on negative transfer in Chap. 2; see also Bardovi-Harlig and Sprouse (2017).

4 RESULTS: COMPONENTS OF INTERCULTURAL COMPETENCE   63

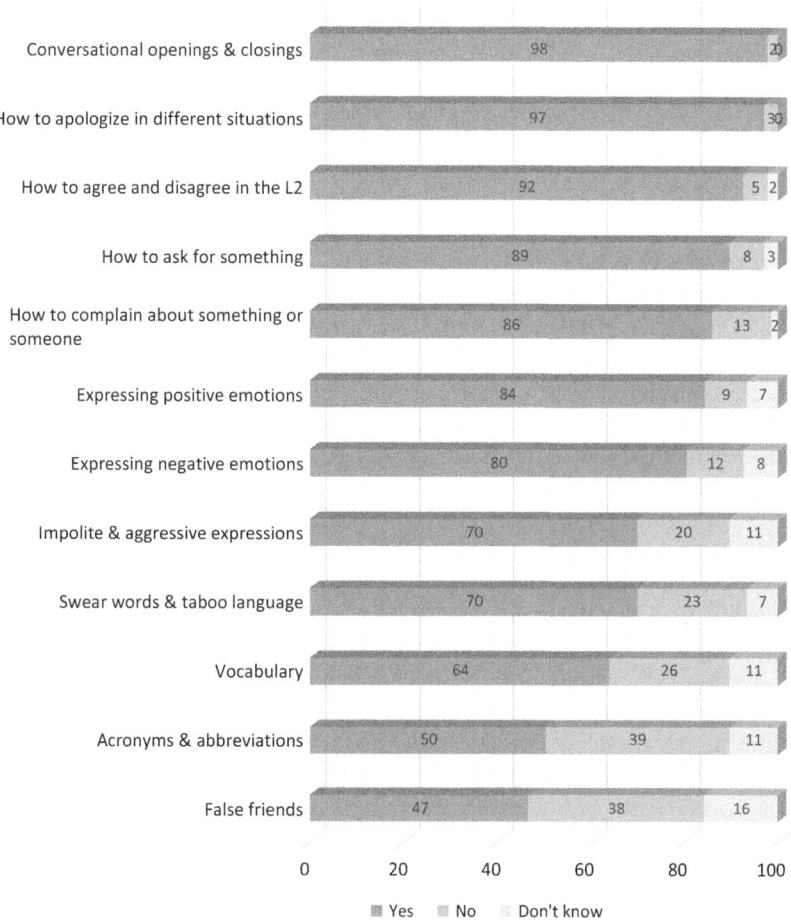

Fig. 4.2 Percentage of teachers who responded *yes*, *no* and *don't know* to whether each linguistic aspect is part of intercultural competence

openings and closings (98%), apologies (97%), (dis)agreements (92%), requests (89%) and complaints (86%). As was seen in Sect. 4.1, the item chosen by the highest number of teachers in responses to question 2 was selected by only 92% of teachers, and the second-ranked item chosen by 87%, the responses to this question demonstrate a very high degree of agreement among the teachers with regard to the inclusion of pragmatics in IC.

The two emotion items, the expression of positive and negative emotions, were selected by 84 and 80% of teachers, respectively, thus indicating that they should also be considered IC components. The two impoliteness items, *impolite and aggressive expressions* and *swear words and taboo language*, were each selected by 70% of the teachers and thus are also considered to part of IC by a large number of teachers. Although aggressive, impolite and taboo language may not be immediately thought of as important aspects when it comes to IC and the teaching of a MFL, pragmaticians have argued for the teaching of impolite language for years (e.g., Felix-Brasdefer & McKinnon, 2016; House, 2015; Morollón Martí, 2022; Mugford, 2008, 2019). Making L2 learners aware of such language not only ensures a broader understanding of cultural norms with regard to what is considered to be negative or unpleasant in the L2 but also enables MFL learners to make informed decisions regarding their personal safety if they are exposed to such language. Teaching aspects of IC will be addressed in more detail in Chap. 5.

Two of the three items in question 3 that are likely to be perceived as purely lexical—*vocabulary* and *acronyms and abbreviations*—were selected as components of intercultural competence by 64 and 50% of teachers, respectively. The final item, *false friends*, was chosen by 47%. Although well-known ICC models that include linguistic aspects, such as the ones by Byram (1997) and Fantini (2019), feature linguistic components (e.g., "linguistic competence" in the former and "target language proficiency" in the latter), these are not always defined or addressed in great detail and could therefore either remain vague for teachers or attract less attention than some of the other components that are often associated with the respective frameworks, such as Byram's savoirs. Chapter 8 addresses the teachers' education and provides information on whether they encountered IC during their own studies and the scholars that they tend to associate with IC; as will be seen there, 44% of teachers encountered IC during their studies and the majority of those associate it with Byram.

In order to examine differences and similarities in teachers' choices depending on the language on which they focused for this study, the responses were analysed according to language group (see Sect. 4.1 or Table 3.1 for further details). Table 4.2 presents the results of this analysis.

The findings show that the item *conversational openings and closings* was chosen by 100% of German, Italian, Spanish, French, Dutch and Swedish teachers and by 96% of the English teachers. This indicates that there is a very broad agreement that these two speech acts are part of

Table 4.2 Percentage of teachers in each language group who selected each potential linguistic aspect as being part of intercultural competence

	Language group							
	E	G	I	Sp	F	D	Sw	Total
Conversational openings and closings (e.g., greetings, "how are you" questions)	96	100	100	100	100	100	100	**98**
How to apologize in different situations	97	100	100	86	100	100	67	**97**
How to agree and disagree in the L2	92	82	100	100	67	100	100	**92**
How to ask for something (e.g., extension, goods, favours)	85	91	100	100	67	100	100	**89**
How to complain about someone or something	92	82	90	86	83	100	67	**86**
Expressing positive emotions (e.g., happiness)	84	73	90	71	83	100	100	**84**
Expressing negative emotions (e.g., sadness, anger)	80	73	90	71	83	100	67	**80**
Impolite & aggressive expressions	67	64	90	71	100	67	67	**70**
Swear words & taboo language	63	64	100	71	100	67	67	**70**
Vocabulary	65	55	70	29	33	100	100	**64**
Acronyms & abbreviations	47	73	50	43	50	67	67	**50**
False friends	44	55	60	29	33	33	67	**47**

Note: Total score represents all teachers of all languages, and so corresponds to the data presented in Fig. 4.2

Key to languages: *E* English, *G* German, *I* Italian, *Sp* Spanish, *F* French, *D* Dutch, *Sw* Swedish

IC. Interestingly, this is also the only item[3] that received agreement scores that are nearly identical across all language groups.

The least chosen component for each of the five language groups represented by more than three teachers—English, German, Italian, Spanish and French—involved items that are likely to be regarded as lexical: *vocabulary* (German: 55%; Spanish: 29%; French: 33%), *acronyms & abbreviations* (Italian: 50%), and *false friends* (English: 44%; German: 55%; Spanish: 29%; French: 33%). As can be seen, three groups (German, Spanish and French) had two items that were weighted equally lowest (i.e., were chosen by the same number of group members). In addition, there were considerable differences in the percentage of group members that chose the least selected item(s), ranging from 55% (German teachers) to 29%

---

[3] See also Spencer-Oatey's (2018) study on the importance of greetings in intercultural encounters and Crozet and Liddicoat (1999) with regard to intercultural L2 teaching.

(Spanish teachers). However, it needs to be remembered that—as addressed in detail in Sect. 4.1—the number of teachers belonging to the individual groups differs substantially.

Another interesting result is that, compared to Table 4.1 which presented the results of the second survey question about the broader potential list of IC components, even the linguistic components that were considered to be IC components by the lowest number of teachers in any group were still selected by more than the lowest ranking items in Table 4.1: the lowest ranking item in Table 4.1 was *efficiency*, chosen by 12% of the English teachers, 9% of the German ones and no teachers from the other groups; while the lowest-ranked item in Table 4.2, *false friends*, was considered to be part of IC by 44% of the English, 55% of the German, 60% of the Italian, 29% of the Spanish, 33 of the French and Dutch and 67% of the Swedish teachers. This further supports the notion that aspects of linguistic competence ought to be prominent components of IC frameworks.

4.3 Summary

This chapter presented the results of questions 2 and 3 of the survey, which focused on the general and linguistic components of IC. While question 2 contained 24 potential components of intercultural competence, representing abilities, knowledge, skills and attitudes or characteristics that teachers could choose from, question 3 concentrated on the linguistic components of intercultural competence and included 12 items representing speech acts, aspects of (im)politeness, emotions and general lexical items.

Section 4.1 presented the results of the second question, which offered a wide variety of different IC options. The findings showed that all items suggested as possible components of intercultural competence were selected by at least some teachers, thus indicating that all of them could feature in an IC framework. The most frequently chosen items were *awareness of different ways of thinking, orientations and values* (selected by 92% of the teachers), followed by *being understanding and sympathetic when encountering cultural differences* (87%) and *knowledge of politeness norms* (84%). The fact that a key component of pragmatics, politeness, was chosen by the third highest number of teachers gives strong support to the inclusion of pragmatic competence as part of IC, especially since the politeness item was also in third place in an earlier study involving 64 teachers of English in primary, secondary and adult education (Schauer, 2022).

The other overtly pragmatics-related item in question 2, *ability to produce situationally appropriate language*, was in sixth place with 77%, while two items that more indirectly addressed pragmatics, *ability to recognize conflicts and deal with conflicts* and *knowledge of gender-neutral language forms*, were chosen by 58% and 45% of the teachers, respectively. Considering the teachers' choices according to the languages they were teaching, the analysis showed that the pragmatic items *ability to produce situationally appropriate language* and *knowledge of politeness norms* revealed a range from 100% (Italian, Dutch) to 67 (Swedish) for the former, and from 100 (Italian, French) to 57 (Spanish) for the latter, each clearly being selected by more than half of the teachers in each language group. Overall, the results emphasize the key role of pragmatics in IC.

Section 4.2 presented the results of question 3, which focused on 12 linguistic items and asked teachers to indicate whether they considered them to be part of IC. Of the 12 items, five referred to speech acts, two referred to the expression of emotions, two addressed impoliteness and three were likely to be identified as vocabulary options. The results showed that the five speech acts were considered to be IC components by the vast majority of the teachers: conversational openings and closings (98%), apologies (97%), (dis)agreements (92%), requests (89%) and complaints (86%). The two impoliteness-related items, *impolite and aggressive expressions*, and *swear words and taboo language*, were each chosen by 70% of the teachers, which again underlines the importance of pragmatic competence as an essential component of IC. The individual group scores of the teachers who had indicated that they were thinking of a particular language when completing the questionnaire or were only teaching one language also lends further support to the inclusion of speech acts and (im)politeness in IC frameworks.

References

American Psychological Association. (2020). *Publication manual of the American Psychology Association: The official guide to APA style* (7th ed.). American Psychological Association.

Bardovi-Harlig, K., & Sprouse, R. A. (2017). Negative versus positive transfer. In J. L. Liontas (Ed.), *The TESOL Encyclopedia of English language teaching*. Wiley. https://doi.org/10.1002/9781118784235.eelt0084

Byram, M. (1997). *Teaching and assessing intercultural communicative competence*. Multilingual Matters.
Byram, M. (2009). Intercultural speaker and the pedagogy of foreign language education. In D. Deardorff (Ed.), *The SAGE handbook of intercultural competence* (pp. 321–332). Sage.
Council of Europe. (2008). *White paper on intercultural dialogue: "Living together as equals in dignity"*. Council of Europe Publishing.
Council of Europe. (2014). *Developing intercultural competence through education*. Council of Europe Publishing.
Crozet, C., & Liddicoat, A. J. (1999). The challenge of intercultural language teaching: Engaging with culture in the classroom. In J. Lo Bianco, A. J. Liddicoat, & C. Crozet (Eds.), *Striving for the third place: Intercultural competence through language education* (pp. 113–126). Language Australia – The National Languages and Literary Institute of Australia.
Deardorff, D. K. (2006). Identification and assessment of intercultural competence as a student outcome of internationalization. *Journal of Studies in International Education, 10*(3), 241–266.
Department of Education and Skills (Ireland). (2017). *Languages connect: Ireland's strategy for foreign languages in education 2017–2026*. Implementation plan. http://www.education.ie/en/Schools-Colleges/Information/Curriculum-and-Syllabus/Foreign-LanguagesStrategy/fs_languages_connect_implementation_plan.pdf
Dewaele, J. M. (2015). British "bollocks" versus American "jerk": Do native British English speakers swear more—Or differently—Compared to American English speakers? *Applied Linguistics Review, 6*(3), 309–339.
Dewaele, J. M. (2016). Thirty shades of offensiveness: L1 and LX English users' understanding, perception and self-reported use of negative emotion-laden words. *Journal of Pragmatics, 94*, 112–127.
Erdocia, I. (2022). Language and culture wars: The far right's struggle against gender-neutral language. *Journal of Language and Politics, 21*(6), 847–866.
Fantini, A. E. (1995). Introduction—Language, culture and world view: Exploring the nexus. *International Journal of Intercultural Relations, 19*(2), 143–153.
Fantini, A. E. (2019). *Intercultural communicative competence in educational exchange: A multinational perspective*. Routledge.
Félix-Brasdefer, C., & McKinnon, S. (2016). Perceptions of impolite behavior in study abroad contexts and the teaching of impoliteness in L2 Spanish. *Journal of Spanish Language Teaching, 3*, 99–113.
Formato, F. (2018). *Gender, discourse and ideology in Italian*. Palgrave.
House, J. (2015). Epilogue: Impoliteness in learning and teaching. In B. Pizziconi & M. A. Locher (Eds.), *Teaching and learning (im)politeness* (pp. 247–254). De Gruyter.

Jackson, J. (2019). Intercultural competence and L2 pragmatics. In N. Taguchi (Ed.), *The Routledge handbook of second language acquisition and pragmatics* (pp. 479–494). Routledge.
KMK. (1996/2013). *Interkulturelle Bildung und Erziehung in der Schule.* https://www.kmk.org/fileadmin/veroeffentlichungen_beschluesse/ 1996/1996_10_25-Interkulturelle-Bildung.pdf
KMK. (2003). *Beschlüsse der Kultusministerkonferenz: Bildungsstandards für die erste Fremdsprache (Englisch/Französisch) für den mittleren Schulabschluss (Jahrgangsstufe 10).* https://www.kmk.org/fileadmin/veroeffentlichungen_ beschluesse/2003/2003_12_04-BS-erste-Fremdsprache.pdf
KMK. (2004). *Beschlüsse der Kultusministerkonferenz: Bildungsstandards für die erste Fremdsprache (Englisch/Französisch) für den Hauptschulabschluss (Jahrgangsstufe 9).* https://www.kmk.org/fileadmin/veroeffentlichungen_ beschluesse/2004/2004_10_15-Bildungsstandards-ersteFS-Haupt.pdf
KMK. (2012). *Beschlüsse: Bildungsstandards für die fortgeführte Fremdsprache (Englisch/Französisch) für die Allgemeine Hochschulreife vom 18.10.2012.* https://www.kmk.org/fileadmin/veroeffentlichungen_beschluesse/ 2012/2012_10_18-Bildungsstandards-Fortgef-FS-Abi.pdf
Liddicoat, A. J., & Scarino, A. (2013). *Intercultural language teaching and learning.* Wiley Blackwell.
McConachy, T., & Liddicoat, A. J. (2022). Introduction: Second language pragmatics for intercultural understanding. In T. McConachy & A. J. Liddicoat (Eds.), *Teaching and learning second language pragmatics for intercultural understanding* (pp. 1–18). Routledge.
Ministry of Education (Ontario, Canada). (2016). *The Ontario curriculum, grades 9 to 12: Classical studies and international languages.* www.edu.gov.on.ca/ eng/curriculum/secondary/classiclang9 12curr.pdf
Morollón Martí, N. (2022). Concept-based instruction for teaching and learning L2 impoliteness. In T. McConachy & A. J. Liddicoat (Eds.), *Teaching and learning second language pragmatics for intercultural understanding* (pp. 126–150). Routledge.
Mugford, G. (2008). How rude! Teaching impoliteness in the second-language classroom. *ELT Journal, 62*(4), 375–384.
Mugford, G. (2019). *Assessing difficult situations in foreign language learning: Confusion, politeness and hostility.* Routledge.
Potts, C., & Schwarz, F. (2008). *Exclamatives and heightened emotion: Extracting pragmatic generalizations from large corpora* [Unpublished manuscript]. University of Massachusetts Amherst.
Rintell, E. M. (1984). But how did you FEEL about that? The learner's perception of emotion in speech. *Applied Linguistics, 5*(3), 255–264.
Savvidou, C., & Economidou-Kogetsidis, M. (2019). Teaching pragmatics: Nonnative speaker teachers' knowledge, beliefs and reported practices. *Intercultural Communication Education, 2*(1), 39–58.

Schauer, G. A. (2022). Intercultural competence and pragmatics in the L2 classroom: Views of in-service EFL teachers in primary, secondary and adult education. In T. McConachy & A. J. Liddicoat (Eds.), *Teaching and learning second language pragmatics for intercultural understanding* (pp. 173–191). Routledge.

Spencer-Oatey, H. (2018). Transformative learning for social integration: Overcoming the challenge of greetings. *Intercultural Education, 29*(2), 301–315.

Ting-Toomey, S., & Dorjee, T. (2015). Intercultural and intergroup communication competence: Toward an integrative perspective. In A. F. Hannawa & B. H. Spitzberg (Eds.), *Communication competence* (pp. 503–538). De Gruyter Mouton.

UNESCO. (2013). *Intercultural competences: Conceptual and operational framework.* https://unesdoc.unesco.org/ark:/48223/pf0000219768

Open Access This chapter is licensed under the terms of the Creative Commons Attribution 4.0 International License (http://creativecommons.org/licenses/by/4.0/), which permits use, sharing, adaptation, distribution and reproduction in any medium or format, as long as you give appropriate credit to the original author(s) and the source, provide a link to the Creative Commons licence and indicate if changes were made.

The images or other third party material in this chapter are included in the chapter's Creative Commons licence, unless indicated otherwise in a credit line to the material. If material is not included in the chapter's Creative Commons licence and your intended use is not permitted by statutory regulation or exceeds the permitted use, you will need to obtain permission directly from the copyright holder.

CHAPTER 5

Results: Aspects of Modern Foreign Language Teaching in Higher Education

5.1 IMPORTANCE OF ACADEMIC AND GENERAL SKILLS AND COMPETENCES

The first question to which the teachers were asked to respond in the survey focused on their evaluation of the importance of general and academic skills in their teaching: *how important is it for you to teach the following skills and competences in L2 language teaching?* This question was included with the aim of establishing a baseline on how similar or dissimilar the teaching contexts of the teachers participating in the study were. Based on my experience as a director of an English for Academic Purposes (EAP) and study skills programme in the United Kingdom, and a director of a language centre in Germany, I anticipated that modern foreign language teachers in higher education everywhere were likely to primarily focus on academic language skills (the four skills of listening, reading, speaking and writing, plus the additional skill of discussing) in their classes. In addition, I was interested in finding out their views on other areas that are not directly related to using the MFL in an academic context, such as general language skills (i.e., the four skills outside of the academic context) and mediation skills. Intercultural aspects were covered by the response item *strategies that equip learners with practical skills for handling intercultural encounters*, while pragmatics was represented by *L2 expressions that can be used to react in an appropriate and sympathetic manner when encountering cultural differences.*

© The Author(s) 2024
G. A. Schauer, *Intercultural Competence and Pragmatics*,
https://doi.org/10.1007/978-3-031-44472-2_5

Table 5.1 Teachers' evaluations of the importance of teaching selected skills and competences in the L2

	Number of teacher responses (and corresponding percentage of teachers)						
	1	2	3	4	5	Don't know	Average
Academic listening skills	6 (5%)	12 (9%)	14 (11%)	52 (39%)	47 (35%)	2 (2%)	3.93
Academic reading skills	4 (3%)	5 (4%)	3 (2%)	48 (36%)	72 (54%)	1 (1%)	4.36
Academic speaking skills	4 (3%)	5 (4%)	13 (10%)	47 (35%)	64 (48%)	0	4.22
Academic writing skills	5 (4%)	5 (4%)	10 (8%)	40 (30%)	73 (55%)	0	4.29
Academic discussion skills	4 (3%)	3 (2%)	19 (14%)	51 (38%)	54 (41%)	1 (1%)	4.13
General language skills	2 (2%)	4 (3%)	9 (7%)	41 (31%)	77 (58%)	0	4.41
L2 expressions[a]	4 (3%)	2 (2%)	10 (8%)	58 (44%)	58 (44%)	1 (1%)	4.24
Mediation skills	4 (3%)	8 (6%)	32 (24%)	47 (35%)	32 (24%)	10 (8%)	3.77
Strategies[b]	6 (5%)	1 (1%)	9 (7%)	56 (42%)	57 (43%)	4 (3%)	4.22

Notes: The items are shown in the order in which they were presented in the survey. The complete wording of all items, including examples that were given, is available in the Appendix of Chap. 3

1 = very unimportant; 2 = unimportant; 3 = neither important nor unimportant; 4 = important; 5 = very important

[a] *L2 expressions that can be used to react in an appropriate and sympathetic manner when encountering cultural differences*; [b] *Strategies that equip the learner with practical skills for handling intercultural encounters*

Question 1 was answered by 133 participants. Table 5.1 presents the number (and percentage) of teachers who rated each skill or competence on each of the five points on a Likert scale (from 1 *very unimportant* to 5 *very important*) or responded with *don't know*.

The three items considered to be very important by the highest number of teachers were *general language skills* (58%), followed by *academic writing skills* (55%) and *academic reading skills* (54%). The top three items were also the only items that were rated to be very important by more than half of the teachers. This was a surprising finding, as I would have expected the teachers to attach the highest importance to academic skills items. I checked the data to see if the selection of very important for *general language skills* was related to the level the teachers were teaching (e.g., if this option was primarily selected by teachers working with beginner-level learners and not by teachers working with advanced learners) but there was no link. There was also no connection to the language taught by the teachers, which suggests that much importance is attached to general language skills by modern foreign language teachers in higher education.

The results also show that all items included in question 1 were considered to be important or very important by more than half of the teachers. Figure 5.1 presents for each individual skill or competence the combined percentages of the teachers who considered it important or very important, and thus schematically illustrates the areas rated highly by the teachers.

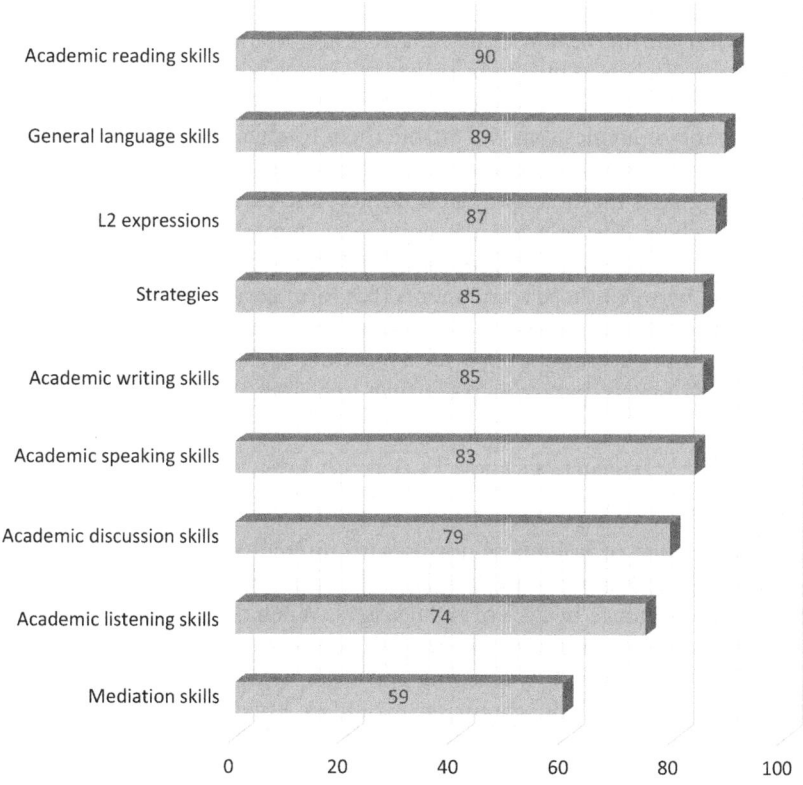

Fig. 5.1 Percentage of teachers who responded that the teaching of each skill or competence in the L2 was very important or important

The percentage of those who consider each skill important and very important reveals that when the two highest-rated Likert scale options are combined, the three highest-ranked items change. While *academic reading skills* (90%) and *general language skills* (89%) have swapped positions but remain in the top three, *academic writing skills* (85%) has been replaced by *appropriate and sympathetic L2 expressions* (87%). This shows that the majority of teachers do not only consider appropriate language to be a part of intercultural competence, as shown in Chap. 4, but that they also consider it important to teach appropriate language in their classrooms; a more detailed analysis and discussion of the pragmatic components that this may refer to is provided in Sect. 5.2, which examines individual linguistic aspects that teachers focus on in their teaching. The combined percentage scores also show that *strategies that equip the learner with practical skills for handling intercultural encounters* are ranked as important or very important by 85% of the teachers. This suggests that the majority of teachers would like to prepare their students for intercultural encounters and provide them with suitable strategies that will enable them to engage in successful intercultural communication. As in the case of appropriate language, the results concerning skills for intercultural encounters also tie in with the high number of teachers who selected the equivalent item as part of intercultural competence in their response to question 2 (see Sect. 4.1). This suggests a direct link between those components that form part of intercultural competence in teachers' views and the issues they address in their own classrooms. In the next section, I provide a more detailed analysis and discussion of linguistic aspects that teachers consider to be important in their teaching.

5.2 Importance of Teaching Language Aspects

The results presented in Sect. 4.1, revealed that 84% of the teachers associated knowledge of politeness norms with intercultural competence, and that situationally appropriate language was considered to be part of intercultural competence by 77% of the teachers. When designing the survey, I was interested in exploring which linguistic aspects teachers considered to be important in their own teaching and whether aspects related to intercultural competence and pragmatics would be rated highly by the teachers or not.

5 RESULTS: ASPECTS OF MODERN FOREIGN LANGUAGE TEACHING... 75

Question 6, answered by all 133 participants, asked *How important is it for you to teach the following language aspects when teaching a foreign language?* Table 5.2 presents the number (and percentage) of teachers who

Table 5.2 Teachers' evaluations of the importance of teaching language aspects

Number of teachers (and corresponding percentage of teachers)

	1	2	3	4	5	Don't know	Average
Acronyms & abbreviations	4 (3%)	10 (8%)	53 (40%)	52 (39%)	13 (10%)	1 (1%)	3.47
Conversational openings and closings	5 (4%)	1 (1%)	8 (6%)	51 (38%)	68 (51%)	0	4.32
Correct pronunciation	3 (2%)	5 (4%)	21 (16%)	66 (50%)	38 (29%)	0	3.98
Expressing negative emotions	4 (3%)	2 (2%)	32 (24%)	63 (47%)	31 (23%)	1 (1%)	3.89
Expressing positive emotions	4 (3%)	1 (1%)	27 (20%)	68 (51%)	32 (24%)	1 (1%)	3.95
False friends	3 (2%)	2 (2%)	38 (29%)	64 (48%)	22 (17%)	4 (3%)	3.84
Grammar	2 (2%)	7 (5%)	12 (9%)	57 (43%)	55 (41%)	0	4.17
How to agree and disagree in the L2	3 (2%)	0	7 (5%)	55 (41%)	68 (51%)	0	4.39
How to apologize	4 (3%)	0	11 (8%)	65 (49%)	52 (39%)	1 (1%)	4.23
How to ask for something	4 (3%)	0	9 (7%)	54 (41%)	65 (49%)	1 (1%)	4.35
How to complain	4 (3%)	0	25 (19%)	61 (46%)	42 (32%)	1 (1%)	4.05
Impolite & aggressive expressions	8 (6%)	12 (9%)	35 (26%)	49 (37%)	26 (20%)	3 (2%)	3.62
Situationally appropriate language	4 (3%)	0	2 (2%)	43 (32%)	82 (62%)	2 (2%)	4.54
Swear words & taboo language	12 (9%)	20 (15%)	41 (31%)	47 (35%)	10 (8%)	3 (2%)	3.24
Everyday life vocabulary	3 (2%)	1 (1%)	9 (7%)	44 (33%)	76 (57%)	0	4.42
Academic vocabulary	4 (3%)	5 (4%)	16 (12%)	47 (35%)	60 (45%)	1 (1%)	4.18
Professional vocabulary	4 (3%)	12 (9%)	39 (29%)	44 (33%)	30 (23%)	4 (3%)	3.72
Out of use vocabulary	29 (22%)	41 (31%)	48 (36%)	10 (8%)	3 (2%)	2 (2%)	2.42
Regional vocabulary	12 (9%)	29 (22%)	30 (23%)	46 (35%)	12 (9%)	4 (3%)	3.22

Notes: The items are shown in the order in which they were presented in the survey. The exact wording of all items, including examples that were provided for them, is given in the Appendix of Chap. 3. Please note that due to the limited space available in the table, some items had to be reworded here, for example, the item *regional vocabulary* in this table was actually "Vocabulary that may only be used in a particular region or country in which the L2 is the official language (e.g., the German "Grüß Gott" [lit. Greet God] in southern Germany and Austria)" in the survey. Due to rounding, different raw numbers may result in the same percentage; for example, 1.52% and 2.29% are both rounded to 2%

1 = very unimportant, 2 = unimportant, 3 = neither important nor unimportant, 4 = important, 5 = very important

rated each language aspect on each of the five points on a Likert rating scale (from 1 *very unimportant* to 5 *very important*) or who responded with *don't know*.

The three items chosen as very important by the highest percentage of teachers were *situationally appropriate language* (62%), followed by *everyday life vocabulary* (57%), and the two speech act items *conversational openings and closings* and *how to agree and disagree* in joint third place (51%). The items in the top three positions were also the only items that were rated to be very important by more than half of the teachers. This illustrates again that pragmatic aspects are assigned importance by modern foreign language teachers in higher education.

The results further show that—in contrast to the items included in question 1 discussed in Sect. 5.1—not all items included in question 6 were considered to be important or very important by more than half of the teachers: *Acronyms and abbreviations* approaches half, with 10% of teachers rating them as very important and 39 as important for a total of 49%; while *regional vocabulary* and *swear words and taboo language* were considered to be at least important by 44% and 43% of the teachers, respectively. The item the majority of the teachers considered to be very unimportant (22%) or unimportant (31%) was *out of use vocabulary*.

Figure 5.2 presents the individual items with the combined percentages of the teachers who considered them either important or very important, and thus schematically illustrates the linguistic aspects that were rated highly by the teachers.

The combined percentage scores show that the top-ranked items that were considered to be very important by the highest percentages of teachers are also in the top three after combining results for very important and important. *Situationally appropriate language* (which achieved a combined score of 94%) was in first place, followed by *how to agree and disagree* (93%). In third place is *everyday life vocabulary*, (90 %), followed by two pragmatic items with 89 per cent each, *how to ask for something* (i.e., requests) and *conversational openings and closings*. Thus, four of the five highest-ranked items are related to L2 learners' pragmatic competence. The remaining speech acts also achieved high combined importance scores: apologies (88%) and complaints (77%).

Regarding items that are part of pragmatics but not based around speech acts, *impolite and aggressive expressions* were considered to be either

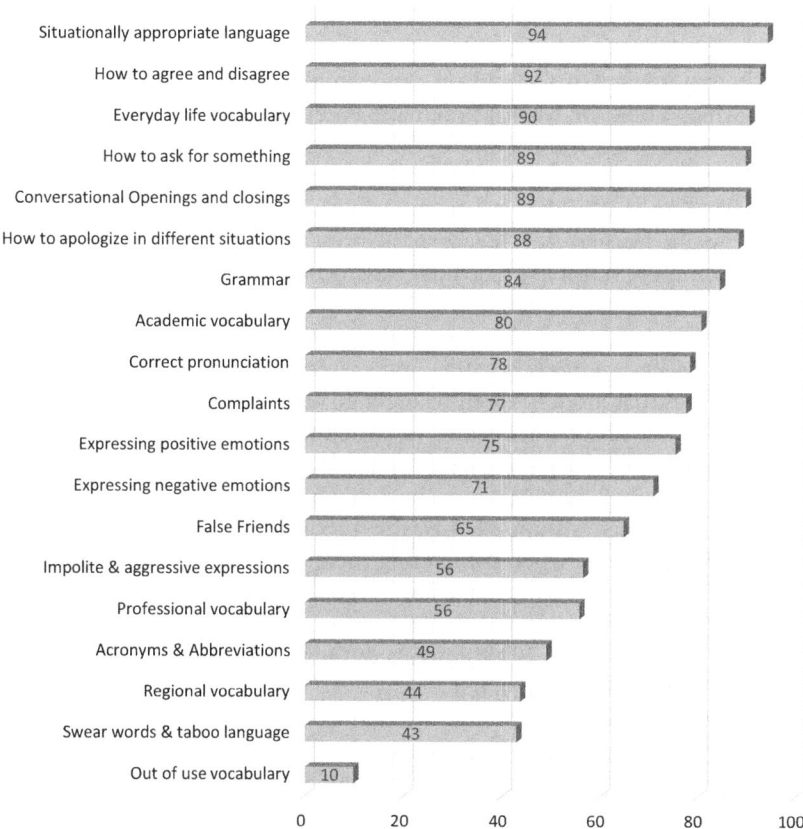

Fig. 5.2 Percentage of teachers who responded that the teaching of each language aspect in the L2 was very important or important

Note: Due to the limited space available in the figure, some items had to be reworded here, for example, the item regional vocabulary in this figure was actually "Vocabulary that may only be used in a particular region or country in which the L2 is the official language (e.g., the German "Grüß Gott" [lit. Greet God] in southern Germany and Austria)" in the survey.

important or very important by 56% of the teachers, while *swear words and taboo language* achieved a combined importance percentage of 43%. These are interesting results, since 70% of the teachers considered these items to be part of intercultural competence, as was shown in Sect. 4.2. Thus, not all items that teachers consider to be part of intercultural competence are also perceived as important when it comes to teaching them.

The two items that focused on expressing positive and negative emotions, which could be part of pragmatic competence, were considered to be important or very important by 75% and 71% of the teachers, respectively. Both items were also considered to be part of intercultural competence (see Sect. 4.2), but in contrast to the aforementioned (im)politeness items, giving learners the means to express their feelings seems to be focused on more in the participants' classrooms.

Apart from vocabulary relating to everyday life, the non-pragmatic items that received the highest combined percentage scores are *grammar* (84%), *academic vocabulary* (80%) and *correct pronunciation* (78%). This demonstrates that modern foreign language teachers at higher educational institutions also attach importance to structural aspects of language.

To obtain a more detailed picture of the importance that MFL teachers attach to individual linguistic aspects, Table 5.3 presents the scores of the individual language groups, that is, the 115 teachers who were focusing on a specific language when completing the questionnaires (see Sect. 3.1). Since four of the groups contain fewer than eight participants—which is considered to be the minimum number for statistical analysis of ordinal data (see Brunner et al., 2018; Jenkins & Quintana-Ascencio, 2020)—no statistical analysis was conducted.

The results reveal that overall, the scores of the individual groups do not tend to differ by more than one point from each other, nor do they differ much from the average score. In the few cases, where the scores of the individual groups differ from another by more than one point, this is likely to be due to the small number of participants in the Dutch and Swedish groups. For example, *how to complain* had a total group score of 3.96, with Italian teachers assigning the highest group score of 4.6 and Dutch and Swedish teachers scoring it 3.33 and 3.67, respectively. The only instance in which differences in the groups' ratings are notable with the larger groups is the item *regionally variable vocabulary* (English: 2.99; German: 4.09; Italian: 3.60; Spanish: 3.43; French: 3.50; Dutch: 1.67; Swedish: 3.00; total group average: 3.19).

This indicates that irrespective of the language they are teaching, modern foreign language teachers in higher education institutions tend to have similar views on the importance of individual linguistic features. The high number of teachers attaching importance to linguistic features that are directly (speech acts, appropriate language, politeness and impoliteness)

Table 5.3 Averages of teachers' evaluations of the importance of teaching individual language aspects, for each language group

	Language							
	English	German	Italian	Spanish	French	Dutch	Swedish	Average
Acronyms & abbreviations	3.45	3.45	3.40	3.86	3.17	3.67	3.33	3.48
Conversational openings and closings	4.15	4.36	4.80	4.14	4.17	4.67	4.33	4.38
Correct pronunciation	3.91	4.18	4.40	3.57	3.83	3.67	4.33	3.98
Expressing negative emotions	3.75	3.73	4.30	3.71	4.00	3.67	4.00	3.88
Expressing positive emotions	3.83	3.82	4.30	3.71	4.00	3.67	4.00	3.91
False friends	3.73	3.64	4.00	4.29	3.67	3.67	3.33	3.76
Grammar	4.07	4.27	4.40	3.86	4.33	4.00	4.67	4.22
How to agree and disagree	4.33	4.45	4.60	4.14	4.17	4.33	4.33	4.33
How to apologize	4.15	4.18	4.60	3.86	4.17	4.00	4.00	4.12
How to ask for something	4.23	4.36	4.60	4.14	4.33	4.33	4.67	4.38
How to complain	3.99	4.00	4.60	3.86	4.33	3.33	3.67	3.96
Impolite and aggressive expressions	3.56	3.64	3.70	3.57	4.00	3.00	3.67	3.57
Situationally appropriate language	4.52	4.55	4.80	4.14	4.50	4.33	4.33	4.46
Swear words and taboo language	3.11	3.18	3.60	3.86	3.67	2.67	2.67	3.25
Everyday life vocabulary	4.25	4.55	4.80	4.14	4.67	4.67	4.67	4.54
Academic vocabulary	4.36	3.64	4.10	3.71	4.33	3.33	3.67	3.87
Professional vocabulary	3.95	3.36	3.20	2.71	3.50	2.67	3.33	3.24
Out of use vocabulary	2.31	2.73	2.50	2.71	2.33	1.67	3.00	2.47
Regional vocabulary	2.99	4.09	3.60	3.43	3.50	1.67	3.00	3.19

Note: The group scores were calculated by adding the scores that individual teachers had assigned to the respective survey item and then dividing them by the total number of teachers in the respective group

1 = very unimportant; 2 = unimportant, 3 = neither important nor unimportant, 4 = important, 5 = very important

or indirectly (e.g., expressing emotions) linked to pragmatics further underlines that pragmatic competence is at the core of L2 teaching. This then also supports the findings of Cohen's (2018) study, which revealed that native and non-native speaker L2 teachers tend to cover a range of pragmatic aspects in their teaching.

This concludes the discussion of linguistic aspects in this chapter. Section 5.3 focuses on non-linguistic components frequently associated with intercultural competence, while Sect. 5.4 addresses the coverage of specific topics that may be associated with intercultural and diversity competence in materials used in the MFL classroom.

5.3 Importance of Teaching Information Pertaining to L2 Countries and Cultures

This section focuses on question 4 of the survey, in which the teachers were asked *How important is it for you to teach the following facts/information about the countries and cultures in which the L2 is an official language or native language?* The question featured 16 items, involving ideas such as different ways of thinking, the arts, biology and ecology, infrastructure and travel, and wars and conflicts, reflecting the diverse components of culture that were discussed in Sect. 2.2 (e.g., CoE, 2014; Jedynak, 2011; Liddicoat & Scarino, 2013; Sercu, 2000), as well as the knowledge components of intercultural competence frameworks (e.g., Byram, 2021). Table 5.4 presents the results from the 133 participants.

The results reveal that there is only one item considered to be very important by more than half of the teachers, namely, *different ways of thinking, orientations and values*, which was rated as very important by 60% of the teachers. The difference in number to the items in second and third positions, *literature, art and music* (27%), and *history* (20%) is striking. Figure 5.3 provides the combined percentage scores of the very important and important ratings by the teachers for the individual items. It illustrates that *different ways of thinking, orientations and values* is not only the item that received the highest number of very important scores but also the item that received the highest number of combined very important and important scores (94%). This is perhaps not surprising,

Table 5.4 Teachers' evaluations of the importance of teaching facts and information about L2 countries and cultures

Number of teachers responses (and corresponding percentage of teachers)

	1	2	3	4	5	Don't know	Average
Biology & ecology	7 (5%)	24 (18%)	70 (53%)	23 (17%)	5 (4%)	3 (2%)	2.96
Celebrations	2 (2%)	7 (5%)	33 (25%)	65 (49%)	23 (17%)	2 (2%)	3.77
Different ways of thinking[a]	3 (2%)	0	3 (2%)	46 (35%)	79 (60%)	1 (1%)	4.51
Economy & finance	3 (2%)	9 (7%)	71 (54%)	41 (31%)	8 (6%)	0	3.32
Geography	2 (2%)	7 (5%)	45 (34%)	66 (50%)	12 (9%)	0	3.60
Healthcare & medicine	5 (4%)	4 (3%)	56 (42%)	50 (38%)	15 (11%)	2 (2%)	3.51
History	2 (2%)	4 (3%)	31 (23%)	68 (52%)	26 (20%)	1 (1%)	3.85
Infrastructure & travel	7 (5%)	12 (9%)	55 (42%)	48 (36%)	10 (8%)	0	3.32
International relations	2 (2%)	5 (4%)	52 (40%)	60 (46%)	11 (8%)	1 (1%)	3.56
Literature, art & music	1 (1%)	4 (3%)	28 (21%)	59 (45%)	35 (27%)	4 (3%)	3.97
Political systems[b]	1 (1%)	7 (5%)	39 (30%)	61 (47%)	21 (16%)	2 (2%)	3.73
Wars & conflicts	3 (2%)	11 (8%)	50 (38%)	51 (39%)	12 (9%)	3 (2%)	3.46
Important national symbols[c]	1 (1%)	13 (10%)	51 (39%)	49 (37%)	16 (12%)	2 (2%)	3.51
Legal system	3 (2%)	12 (9%)	64 (49%)	40 (31%)	11 (8%)	1 (1%)	3.34
Religious communities[d]	2 (2%)	6 (5%)	40 (30%)	66 (50%)	17 (13%)	1 (1%)	3.69
Well-known individuals[e]	4 (3%)	4 (3%)	50 (38%)	53 (40%)	22 (17%)	0	3.64

Note: The complete wording of all items including examples given is available in the appendix of Chap. 3

1 = very unimportant, 2 = unimportant, 3 = neither important nor unimportant, 4 = important, 5 = very important

[a]*Different ways of thinking, orientations and values*; [b]*political systems & structures*; [c]*important national symbols & flags*; [d]*religious communities & religious symbols, holidays*, etc.; [e]*well-known individuals of the target country*

since the expression "different ways of thinking" is mentioned in the introduction of Byram's (2009) handbook chapter on communicative competence and in the Council of Europe's (2012) publication, while "values" feature frequently in Byram's work (e.g., Byram, 2021) and both "values" and "orientations" are frequently referred to in the publications by the Council of Europe (e.g., CoE, 2012, 2014). Thus, if teachers are looking for literature on the subject of intercultural competence, they are likely to encounter these terms.

The items that were selected by the second and third highest number of teachers as being very important—*literature, art and music* and *history*—also rate highly in the analysis combining responses of important and very important, although they now share a joint second place with 71%. This result ties in with Sercu's (2000, p. 28) definition of culture that distinguishes "small *c*" and "big *C*" components and explicitly lists "history, […], literature […] and artistic products" as representatives of big *C* culture.

Figure 5.3 also shows that nine of the 16 items were considered to be either important or very important by more than half of the teachers,

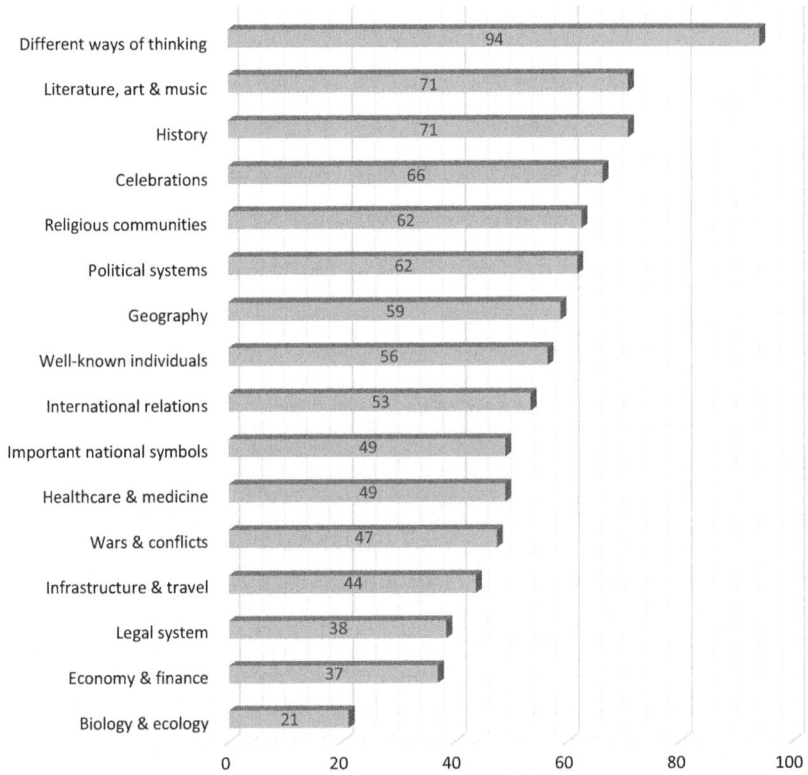

Fig. 5.3 Percentage of teachers who responded that the teaching of facts relating to L2 countries and cultures was very important or important

while three (*important national symbols and flags, healthcare and medicine and wars and conflicts*) approached the halfway mark. While three of the four lowest-ranked items could be regarded to be of relevance to particular learner groups but potentially not all learners (*infrastructure and travel, legal system, economy and finance*), I was surprised at the low rating for *biology and ecology*, which received the lowest combined importance and highest combined unimportance scores (21% and 23%, respectively). Given the very notable and widely reported droughts, periods of hot weather and severe weather conditions the world has experienced in recent years and the effects this has had on agriculture, general food supply and water reserves in many countries, I would have expected this item to score more highly. However, perhaps the terms chosen for this item were not sufficiently precise, and a different choice—such as a combination of *agriculture, the environment* and *sustainability*—would have led to different results.

An alternative reason that came to mind for the low importance of *biology and ecology* was that perhaps the language the teachers were teaching could play a role with regard to that rating. For example, if teachers used newspaper articles or streamed news channels in their teaching, this could potentially impact their views on the importance of these issues, especially if they received wide media attention. To explore whether teachers focusing on different languages when they were completing the questionnaire might have had an impact on their ratings, I analysed the data for the respective language groups, and this is presented in Table 5.5. As noted previously, the group sizes differ considerably and therefore no statistical analysis was conducted. In addition, scores from the two groups that consist of only three teachers each (Dutch and Swedish) will not be commented on here if they deviate markedly from the other groups.

1 = very unimportant; 2 = unimportant, 3 = neither important nor unimportant, 4 = important, 5 = very important.

The results of the individual teacher groups indicate broad agreement regarding the top-ranked item, *different ways of thinking, orientations and values*, as the group scores cluster close to the average. However, the group scores also indicate differences in other items based on the language taught. For example, the Italian teachers rated *geography* more highly than the other groups, 4.40 compared to 3.28 from the English teachers. In the case of *literature, art and music*, the scores of the English and German teachers differed by more than one point, 3.41 and 4.64, respectively. The scores of the English and Spanish teachers approach a one-point difference in the category of *wars and conflict*, 3.01 and 4.00, respectively.

Table 5.5 Averages of teachers' evaluations of the importance of teaching facts and information about the L2 countries and cultures, for each language group

	Language							
	English	German	Italian	Spanish	French	Dutch	Swedish	Average
Biology & ecology	2.72	3.64	3.00	2.57	2.50	2.67	3.33	2.91
Celebrations	3.42	3.82	4.20	3.71	3.67	4.00	4.67	3.93
Different ways of thinking	4.32	4.45	4.70	4.43	4.50	4.67	4.67	4.54
Economy & finance	3.20	3.27	3.30	3.57	3.33	3.33	3.33	3.33
Geography	3.28	3.82	4.40	3.86	3.50	3.67	4.00	3.79
Healthcare & medicine	3.28	3.45	3.40	3.71	3.50	4.00	3.33	3.52
History	3.49	4.27	4.50	4.14	3.67	3.00	4.00	3.86
Infrastructure & travel	3.12	3.64	3.70	2.86	3.33	3.33	3.00	3.28
International relations	3.30	3.82	3.60	3.43	3.83	3.00	3.67	3.51
Literature, art & music	3.41	4.64	4.40	4.29	3.83	3.67	4.00	4.03
Political systems & structures	3.32	4.18	4.00	3.57	3.83	4.00	3.67	3.78
Wars & conflicts	3.01	3.55	3.70	4.00	3.50	3.33	3.33	3.45
Important national symbols	3.24	3.55	3.80	3.86	3.67	2.67	3.67	3.50
Legal system	3.17	3.27	3.10	3.71	3.17	2.00	3.33	3.11
Religion	3.42	3.73	4.10	4.14	3.17	3.67	3.33	3.64
Well-known individuals	3.51	3.82	4.20	3.43	3.50	3.00	3.67	3.58

Note: The group scores were calculated by adding the scores that individual teachers had assigned to the respective survey item and then dividing them by the total number of teachers in the respective group

It is interesting that the German teachers scored the item *biology and ecology* the highest, with the rating 3.64, more than one point higher than the French (2.50) and Spanish (2.57) teachers. In order to find out if media coverage of issues related to climate change differed considerably across media in the respective languages or if the term chosen for the item may not have worked well across all languages, additional research would be necessary that explored potential reasons for the rating. This example also illustrates that future large-scale studies that could explore differences in L2 teachers' views based a variety of different variables would be advantageous, as they could help shed light on differences and similarities in modern foreign language teaching. With items that may be ambiguous, such as *biology and ecology*, it would be helpful to either conduct pilot studies with individuals representing a variety of L2s, or to ask participants for email addresses in the main study to be able to contact them in order to discuss cases like this.

This concludes the discussion of the importance that teachers assigned to specific areas that could be associated with culture and intercultural competence. In the next section, the focus is on texts and materials.

5.4 Importance of Materials and Texts Covering Specific Topics

This section analyses responses to question 5 of the survey, which focused on materials and texts and asked the teachers *How important is it for you to include the following [texts and materials] in your language classes?* The question featured 11 items covering issues such as culture shock, study abroad, and diversity. As I noted in Chap. 2 when presenting different definitions for culture, culture is not seen as monolithic but rather as multifaceted, representing values and lived experiences of a very diverse and heterogenous group of individuals (see, e.g., Liddicoat & Scarino, 2013; CoE, 2014). In their definition of culture, Liddicoat and Scarino (2013) refer to a number of factors commonly associated with diversity, such as age, gender, religion, ethnicity and sexuality.[1] Their definition and recent publications addressing diversity issues in foreign language teaching (e.g., Blackburn et al., 2018; Dellenty, 2019; Liddicoat, 2009; Mills & Mustapha, 2015; Paiz, 2020; Pakuła, 2021), as well as my own professional experiences with culture shock and study abroad as director of the EAP Programme at Lancaster, inspired this question. Table 5.6 presents the responses from the 133 participants.

---

[1] Interestingly, these factors match the components of diversity charters developed and signed by representatives of EU countries and supported by the European Commission (n.d.). Although the primary purpose of these charters is to raise awareness of diversity issues in institutions and improve working conditions for diverse workforces, the diversity components of the individual charters nevertheless indicate that the representatives signing them acknowledge that diversity factors exist and should be considered in their workplace culture. The considerable number of signatories throughout the European Union then supports the notion that cultures are seen as representing diverse groups of individuals.

Table 5.6 Teachers' evaluations of the importance of materials and texts covering specific topics

Number of teacher responses (and corresponding percentage of teachers)

	1	2	3	4	5	Don't know	Average
Materials—culture shock[a]	2 (2%)	6 (5%)	44 (33%)	49 (37%)	32 (24%)	0	3.77
Materials—age groups[b]	4 (3%)	10 (8%)	51 (38%)	52 (39%)	14 (11%)	2 (2%)	3.47
Materials—countries[c]	1 (1%)	5 (4%)	34 (26%)	62 (47%)	26 (20%)	3 (2%)	3.84
Texts—males and females[d]	4 (3%)	7 (5%)	35 (26%)	46 (35%)	39 (30%)	2 (2%)	3.83
Newspaper articles[e]	5 (4%)	5 (4%)	33 (25%)	59 (44%)	27 (20%)	4 (3%)	3.76
Texts—religious beliefs[f]	7 (5%)	15 (11%)	42 (32%)	44 (33%)	19 (14%)	5 (4%)	3.42
Texts—immigrants[g]	3 (2%)	4 (3%)	33 (25%)	53 (40%)	38 (29%)	1 (1%)	3.91
Texts—disabilities[h]	1 (1%)	7 (5%)	50 (38%)	49 (37%)	24 (18%)	1 (1%)	3.67
Texts—LGBTIQ[i]	4 (3%)	11 (8%)	49 (37%)	38 (29%)	25 (19%)	5 (4%)	3.54
Texts—study abroad[j]	2 (2%)	1 (1%)	26 (20%)	54 (41%)	49 (37%)	0	4.11
Texts—ethnic backgrounds[k]	3 (2%)	3 (2%)	27 (20%)	58 (44%)	41 (31%)	1 (1%)	3.99

Note:

1 = very unimportant, 2 = unimportant, 3 = neither important nor unimportant, 4 = important, 5 = very important

[a]*Materials focusing on culture shock;* [b]*materials focusing on different age groups;* [c]*materials written by individuals from different countries;* [d]*equal representation of texts focusing on males and females;* [e]*newspaper articles originating from newspapers that differ with regard to their political views;* [f]*texts addressing the experiences and views of individuals with different religious beliefs;* [g]*texts addressing the experience of immigrants;* [h]*texts addressing the experience of individuals with disabilities;* [i]*texts addressing LGBTIQ issues;* [j]*texts addressing study abroad experiences;* [k]*texts representing the views or experience of individuals with different ethnic backgrounds*

The three items considered to be very important by the highest number of teachers were *texts addressing study abroad experiences* (37%), followed by *texts representing the views or experience of individuals with different ethnic backgrounds* (31%) and *equal representation of texts focusing on males and females* (30%). In contrast to the top three items in Sect. 5.3, the top three items in Table 5.6 are relatively close together with regard to their percentage scores. They also suggest that the modern foreign language teachers attach importance to issues that are likely to be highly relevant to their own students' academic lives, such as study abroad sojourns, as well as issues that are of a broader societal and cultural relevance. To obtain a fuller picture of the items considered to be either very important or important by the teachers, Fig. 5.4 presents the combined percentages of the teachers who scored the individual items with one of these two ratings.

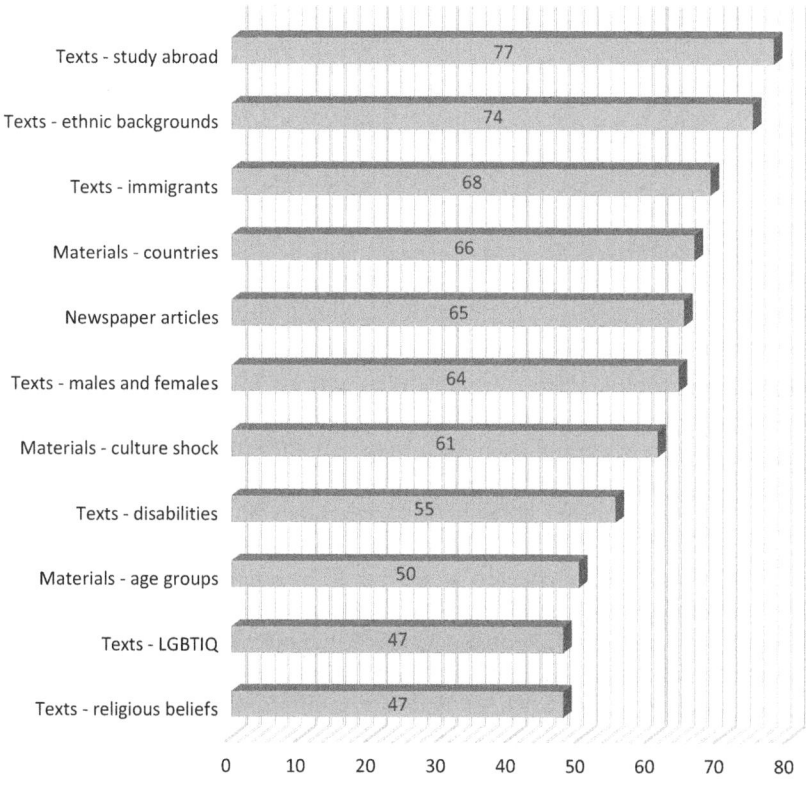

Fig. 5.4 Percentage of teachers who responded that materials and texts covering each specific topic was very important or important

Analysis of the combined very important and important scores shows that—like with the percentage scores in Table 5.6 for the items considered very important—there is relatively little difference between the top-scored items. Two of the top three items according to the very important scores, *texts addressing study abroad experiences* (77%) and *texts representing the views or experience of individuals with different ethnic backgrounds* (74%), are also in top positions in the combined importance analysis. The item in third place is different, however, *texts addressing the experience of immigrants* (68%) which replaced *equal representation of texts focusing on males and females* in the former top three.

The findings also show that the majority of the questionnaire items for this question were considered to be important or very important by more than half of the teachers. While two items—*texts addressing LGBTIQ issues* and *texts addressing the experiences and views of individuals with different religious beliefs* (both 47%)—fall short of the halfway mark, they are close to it. Thus, the findings suggest that the teachers consider it important to expose their MFL learners to a wide variety of texts and materials that present different perspectives and also address a wide range of issues. While equipping L2 learners at university with the necessary language and academic skills needed to navigate the academic context is highly important, the teachers' scores indicate that they are not restricting themselves to academic topics. Instead, they aim to address broader issues that will enable their students to encounter topics that are of cultural and societal relevance, thereby raising their awareness of issues that they may encounter during sojourns in the target country or in conversations with members of the target culture. Reading these texts may not only raise awareness of specific issues and topics, but is also an opportunity to teach vocabulary items that may not be covered in textbooks at schools but that students may encounter during study abroad sojourns, such as "allergy-free lunch tables", "mobility aids", "equal marriage", "gender-neutral/sensitive language", "preferred pronouns" or "the Windrush Generation".

To explore whether teachers focusing on different languages rated the importance of items differently or similarly, the data were again analysed for the individual language groups, as seen in Table 5.7. As in the previous analyses, instances in which the language groups that consisted only of three teachers (Dutch and Swedish) differed considerably from the other groups will not be discussed in detail.

The most striking finding of this analysis is that the Spanish teachers' scores indicate that on average they considered all items to be either

Table 5.7 Averages of teachers' evaluations of the importance of materials and texts covering specific topics, for each language group

	Language							
	English	German	Italian	Spanish	French	Dutch	Swedish	Average
Materials—culture shock	3.75	3.55	3.90	4.43	4.00	3.00	3.33	3.70
Materials—age groups	3.28	3.55	3.70	4.14	3.50	2.67	3.33	3.46
Materials—countries	3.67	3.55	3.40	4.71	4.00	2.33	3.00	3.54
Texts—males and females	3.77	3.36	3.80	4.57	4.00	3.33	3.33	3.76
Newspaper articles	3.51	3.82	3.70	4.14	4.33	3.00	4.00	3.79
Texts—religious beliefs	3.08	3.73	3.10	4.43	3.50	1.67	3.00	3.22
Texts—immigrants	3.61	4.18	4.50	4.71	3.50	4.33	3.00	3.99
Texts—disabilities	3.48	3.73	4.00	4.43	3.33	3.00	2.67	3.53
Texts—LGBTIQ	3.21	3.55	3.50	4.57	3.33	3.67	1.67	3.37
Texts—study abroad	3.95	4.09	4.30	4.71	4.00	3.00	3.67	3.96
Texts—ethnic backgrounds	3.85	3.91	4.00	4.71	4.00	3.67	3.00	3.89

Note: The group scores were calculated by adding the scores that individual teachers had assigned to the respective survey item and then dividing them by the total number of teachers in the respective group
1 = very unimportant; 2 = unimportant, 3 = neither important nor unimportant, 4 = important, 5 = very important

important or very important, since their lowest score is 4.14 (*materials focusing on different age groups*) and their highest 4.71, which applies to four different items. The Dutch and Swedish teachers have some of the lowest ratings (e.g., 1.67 for *texts addressing the experiences and views of individuals with different religious beliefs* in case of the Dutch teachers and the same score for *texts addressing LGBTIQ issues* in case of the Swedish teachers). However, as mentioned above, it needs to be borne in mind that these groups only comprised three teachers each.

Considering the five languages that were represented by more than three teachers, the data show that there are few instances of those groups' scores deviating by more than one point. One of these instances concerns the items on different religious beliefs. Here, the English and Italian scores

(3.08 and 3.10, respectively) differ markedly from the Spanish score of 4.43. Regarding *texts addressing the experience of immigrants*, the English (3.61) and French (3.50) scores are markedly lower than those of the Italian (4.50) and Spanish (4.71) teachers. The Spanish teachers also score the item relating to LGBTIQ texts considerably higher (4.57) than the other teacher groups. It would be interesting to explore further why the Spanish teachers felt comparatively strongly about all items in this question. They were an all-female group with varying years of teaching experience, completed their degrees in either Spain or Mexico, represented various age groups and were all teaching outside of a Spanish-speaking country. Thus, the background section of the questionnaire did not yield any insights into why their scores differed from the others. This suggests that, as had been mentioned previously, further studies may benefit from a methodology that allows participants to leave contact details if they are happy to take part in a follow-up investigation in order to explore these issues.

5.5 Summary

This chapter presented the analysis and discussion of questions 1, 4, 5 and 6 of the survey, all of which related to various aspects of teaching. Section 5.1 addressed question 1, which asked teachers to rate the importance of nine skills and competences on a five-point Likert scale. The question featured nine items that predominantly focused on academic skills but also addressed pragmatic and intercultural aspects. The results revealed that the top three items that had been rated as very important by the teachers were *general language skills* (58%), *academic writing skills* (55%) and *academic reading skills* (54%). These top three items were also the only items that were rated to be very important by more than half of the teachers. The combined analysis of the very important and important scores showed that two of the three top items considered to be very important were also in the top three in the combined ranking, namely, *academic reading skills* (90%) and *general language skills* (89%), although their order was reversed. The new item in third place was *appropriate and sympathetic L2 expressions* (87%), highlighting the importance attached to pragmatics by the teachers.

Section 5.2 focused on question 6, which asked *How important is it for you to teach the following language aspects when teaching a foreign language?* This question included 19 items covering pragmatic as well as non-pragmatic aspects. The three items considered to be very important by the highest percentage of teachers were *situationally appropriate language* (62%), followed by *everyday life vocabulary* (57%), and the two speech act items *conversational openings and closings* and *how to agree and disagree* in joint third place (51%). These items were also the only items that were rated to be very important by more than half of the teachers. The fact that three of the four items can be categorized as pragmatic again supports the notion that pragmatics is a key component not only of intercultural competence but also of modern foreign language instruction in higher education. The combined very important and important percentage score revealed that the top-ranked items largely remain the same, with the speech act of requests joining the third-placed items: *situationally appropriate language* (94%), *agreeing and disagreeing* (92%), and then *everyday life vocabulary (90%)*, followed by two pragmatic items with 89 % each: *how to ask for something* (i.e., requests) and *conversational openings and closings*. The combined importance rating of the pragmatic items further underscores their significance for MFL teaching. The results of the language group analyses revealed that, overall, the scores of the individual groups did not tend to differ by more than one point from each other, nor did they differ much from the average score. However, as mentioned throughout, it needs to be acknowledged that the group sizes of the individual teacher groups differed considerably.

Section 5.3 addressed question 4, which asked *How important is it for you to teach the following facts/information about the countries and cultures in which the L2 is an official language or native language?* The question comprised 16 items covering a variety of non-linguistic aspects. The results revealed that there was only one item that was considered to be very important by more than half of the teachers: *different ways of thinking, orientations and values* (60%). The difference between this and the items in second and third positions, *literature, art and music* (27%), and *history* (20%) was striking. *Different ways of thinking, orientations and values* was not only the item that received the highest number of very important scores, it is also the item that received the highest number of combined scores (94%). The items ranked second and third highest in the individual very important category remain the same in the combined important and very important category—*literature, art and music* and *history* (now sharing a joint second place with 71%). The analysis of the individual teacher group scores indicated broad agreement regarding the top-ranked item *different ways of thinking, orientations and values*, as the group scores cluster close to the average. However, the group scores also indicated differences depending on the language taught (e.g., in the items *biology and ecology, geography* and *literature, art and music)*. What is notable about the results in this section, however, is the way that the teachers consistently scored *different ways of thinking, orientations and values* highly, an item that is closely related to intercultural competence.

Section 5.4 focused on question 5, which asked *How important is it for you to include the following [texts and materials] in your language classes?* The question contained 11 items covering a variety of content areas. The three items considered to be very important by the highest number of teachers were: *texts addressing study abroad experiences* (37%), *texts representing the views or experience of individuals with different ethnic backgrounds* (31%) and *equal representation of texts focusing on males and females* (30%).Two of the top three items according to the very important scores, *texts addressing study abroad experiences* (77%) and *texts representing the views or experience of individuals with different ethnic backgrounds* (74%), are also in first and second place in the combined importance analysis. However, in the combined importance analysis, the item in third place is different: *texts addressing the experience of immigrants* (68%).

The combined importance scores also showed that the majority of the questionnaire items for this question were considered to be important or very important by more than half of the teachers. The analysis of the language group scores showed that the Spanish teachers considered all items to be either important or very important, with average scores ranging from 4.14 (*materials focusing on different age groups*) to 4.71 (*texts addressing the experience of immigrants*). In contrast, the Dutch and Swedish teachers have some of the lowest ratings. However, as mentioned above, the Dutch and Swedish groups each consisted of only three teachers. In the data of the five languages that were represented by more than three teachers, there are few instances of the group scores deviating by more than one point.

This concludes Chap. 5. Chapter 6 focuses on question 7 of the survey, which explicitly addresses the link between intercultural and pragmatic competence.

References

Blackburn, M. V., Clark, C. T., & Martino, W. J. (Eds.). (2018). *Queer and trans perspectives on teaching LGBT-themed texts in schools*. Routledge.
Brunner, E., Bathke, A. C., & Konietschke, F. (2018). *Rank- and pseudo-rank procedures for independent observations in factorial designs: Using R and SAS*. Springer.

Byram, M. (2009). Intercultural speaker and the pedagogy of foreign language education. In D. Deardorff (Ed.), *The SAGE handbook of intercultural competence* (pp. 321–332). Sage.
Byram, M. (2021). *Teaching and assessing intercultural communicative competence revisited* (2nd ed.). Multilingual Matters.
Cohen, A. D. (2018). *Learning pragmatics from native and nonnative language teachers*. Multilingual Matters.
Council of Europe. (2012). *Intercultural competence for all: Preparation for living in a heterogenous world*. Council of Europe Publishing.
Council of Europe. (2014). *Developing intercultural competence through education*. Council of Europe Publishing.
Dellenty, S. (2019). *Celebrating difference: A whole school approach to LGBT+ inclusion*. Bloomsbury.
European Commission. (n.d.). *EU platform of diversity charters*. https://commission.europa.eu/strategy-and-policy/policies/justice-and-fundamental-rights/combatting-discrimination/tackling-discrimination/diversity-and-inclusion-initiatives/eu-platform-diversity-charters_en
Jedynak, M. (2011). The attitudes of English language teachers towards developing intercultural communicative competence. In J. Arabski & A. Wojtaszek (Eds.), *Aspects of culture in second language acquisition and foreign language learning* (pp. 63–76). Springer.
Jenkins, D. G., & Quintana-Ascencio, P. F. (2020). A solution to minimum sample size for regressions. *PLoS ONE, 15*(2), e0229345. https://doi.org/10.1371/journal.pone.0229345.
Liddicoat, A. J. (2009). Sexual identity as linguistic failure: Trajectories of interaction in the heteronormative language classroom. *Journal of Language, Identity and Education, 8*(2/3), 191–202.
Liddicoat, A. J., & Scarino, A. (2013). *Intercultural language teaching and learning*. Wiley Blackwell.
Mills, S., & Mustapha, A. S. (Eds.). (2015). *Gender representations in learning materials: International perspectives*. Routledge.
Paiz, J. M. (2020). *Queering the English language classroom: A practical guide for teachers*. Equinox.
Pakuła, L. (Ed.). (2021). *Linguistic perspectives on sexuality in education: Representations*. Palgrave.
Sercu, L. (2000). *Acquiring intercultural communicative competence from textbooks: The case of Flemish adolescent pupils learning German*. Leuven University Press.

Open Access This chapter is licensed under the terms of the Creative Commons Attribution 4.0 International License (http://creativecommons.org/licenses/by/4.0/), which permits use, sharing, adaptation, distribution and reproduction in any medium or format, as long as you give appropriate credit to the original author(s) and the source, provide a link to the Creative Commons licence and indicate if changes were made.

The images or other third party material in this chapter are included in the chapter's Creative Commons licence, unless indicated otherwise in a credit line to the material. If material is not included in the chapter's Creative Commons licence and your intended use is not permitted by statutory regulation or exceeds the permitted use, you will need to obtain permission directly from the copyright holder.

CHAPTER 6

Results: The Relationship Between Intercultural and Pragmatic Competence

6.1 Teachers' Familiarity with Pragmatic Competence

Previous studies have shown that not all foreign or second language teachers are familiar with the term *pragmatics*, even though some of them may be familiar with components or aspects of it (Glaser, 2018; Savvidou & Economidou-Kogetsidis, 2019; see also Usó Juan & Martínez Flor, 2021). I, therefore, decided to first ask the MFL teachers who participated in this study if they were familiar with pragmatic competence in question 7a before asking them about the link between pragmatic and intercultural competence. Teachers were given three possible answers: *yes*, *no* and *don't know*. In addition, teachers could opt out of answering the question. Of the 133 MFL teachers, 132 provided an answer, while one opted out. Figure 6.1 shows the answers of the 132 teachers regarding their familiarity with pragmatic competence.

The results reveal that 68% of the teachers stated that they were familiar with pragmatic competence, while 18% were not familiar with it and 14% chose the *don't know* option. This means that the majority of teachers indicated that they knew the term. This was a somewhat unexpected finding, since although the first studies in interlanguage pragmatics was published in the late 1970s and early 1980s (e.g., Blum-Kulka, 1980; House, 1982; Kasper, 1981; Olshtain & Cohen, 1983), pragmatics is still regarded to be "a relative latecomer to the field of ISLA [instructed second language

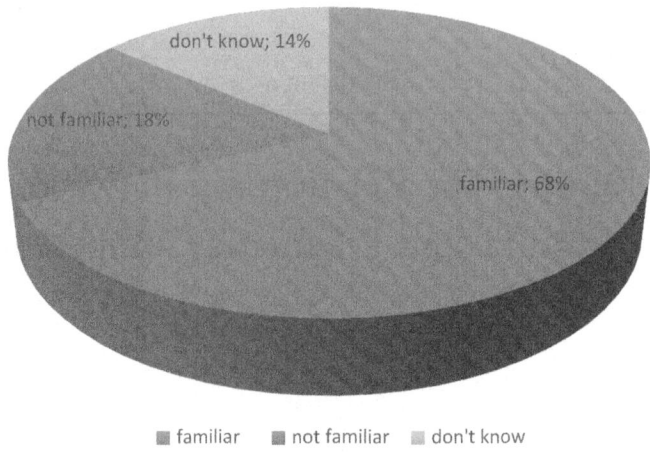

Fig. 6.1 Teachers' familiarity with pragmatic competence (as a percentage of all teachers who responded)

Table 6.1 Teachers' familiarity with pragmatic competence according to language group

	English	German	Italian	Spanish	French	Dutch	Swedish
Yes	50 (68%)	8 (73%)	7 (70%)	6 (86%)	1 (17%)	1 (33%)	2 (67%)
No	16 (22%)	2 (18%)	1 (10%)	1 (14%)	3 (50%)	2 (67%)	0
Don't know	8 (11%)	1 (9%)	2 (20%)	0	2 (33%)	0	1 (33%)

Note: One of the English teachers opted out of answering this question, so there are only 74 participants in the data for the English group here

acquisition]" (Bardovi-Harlig, 2017, p. 226), and thus may not necessarily be addressed in teacher training programmes or covered in literature on MFL teaching written in languages other than English. For this reason, I checked the data to see if teachers' years of teaching experience, the country in which they had obtained their degrees or their age were factors that affected their familiarity with pragmatic competence but there was no connection. I then explored if there was a connection between the language the teachers were focused on when completing the survey and their familiarity with pragmatic competence (i.e., was this topic perhaps focused on more in one L2 teaching community than another?). Table 6.1 presents teachers' familiarity with pragmatic competence depending on the language they taught (see Sect. 3.1 for details of these language groups).

The group results reveal that there are teachers in all MFL groups that stated that they were familiar with pragmatic competence. This suggests that there are no MFL teaching communities that are entirely unfamiliar with the term. However, it once again needs to be acknowledged that the sample size is rather small in total and even more so with respect to some of the language groups. In addition, teachers taking part in the survey are likely to be highly interested in aspects of L2 language teaching and learning and are therefore perhaps more aware of technical terms and areas in foreign and second language teaching than the L2 higher education teaching community as a whole.

Due to the different sizes of the language groups, not much can be said about the percentage distribution regarding teachers' familiarity with pragmatic competence. However, it is interesting that out of the mid-sized groups comprising 11 to 6 teachers, the German, Italian and Spanish teachers were more familiar with it than the French ones. This could be related to literature available on the topic in the respective languages. While researchers have investigated aspects of Spanish pragmatics for years and also published in Spanish (e.g., Placencia & Bravo, 2002; Félix-Brasdefer, 2018) and done the same for a number of years in Italian (for an overview, see Nuzzo & Santoro, 2017), the same may still not be the case in French.[1] In German, contrastive studies of German and English pragmatics were conducted early on and also reported in German-language publications (e.g., House, 1997), and a number of introductory volumes in German exist (e.g., Finkbeiner, 2015; Maibauer, 2001).

Thus, larger-scale studies that comprise a higher number of modern foreign language teachers teaching a variety of different L2s are needed to explore teachers' understandings with regard to pragmatics in more detail. It would be advantageous if these studies were to offer survey or other data collection methods in a variety of languages, so that language teachers who do not feel comfortable completing a survey in English could also easily take part. Ideally, these studies ought to also ask teachers to provide

---

[1] Almost 20 years ago, in a monograph on Austrian German learners of French, Warga (2004) noted a distinct lack of interlanguage pragmatic studies focusing on French as a L2. Other scholars working on French pragmatics, such as Christine Béal or Celeste Kinginger, seem to have predominantly published in English, based on the information available on their websites.

their own definitions of pragmatic competence in order to examine to what extent teachers' conceptualizations of it converge or diverge. In the present study, asking teachers for a definition was not feasible for a variety of reasons. The most important of these is that for the purposes of the present study, it was important to supply teachers with a single definition of pragmatic competence in order to ensure that they all had a standardized definition for question 7b that would allow them to answer how they perceived the link between pragmatic competence and intercultural competence, addressed in the following section.

6.2 Teachers' Views on the Relationship Between Intercultural and Pragmatic Competence

Here I focus on how MFL teachers view the relationship between intercultural competence and pragmatic competence, the very core of the present research project. As mentioned in Chap. 1 and discussed in more detail in Chap. 2, the link between pragmatic competence and intercultural (communicative) competence tends to be very clear for pragmaticians (e.g., Jackson, 2019; Maier, 2003; McConachy & Liddicoat, 2022; Taguchi & Roever, 2017), but may be less clear for scholars working in the field of IC who are either not very familiar with pragmatics or indeed completely unfamiliar with it (see Spencer-Oatey, 2010). Taguchi and Roever (2017, p. 261) argue that "pragmatic competence in intercultural settings can be viewed as a constituent of intercultural competence" but also acknowledge that "we need more studies that examine the relationship between pragmatic competence and intercultural competence". In developing the survey for the present research, my own view was that pragmatic competence is part of intercultural competence, and I was interested in finding out whether the teachers would share this view or have completely different notions. The question addressing the link between pragmatic and intercultural competence was deliberately placed towards the end of the survey after teachers had already reflected on other questions that addressed potential features and components of intercultural competence.

Question 7b stated the following: *For the purposes of this questionnaire, pragmatic competence in an L2 will be defined as a person's ability to communicate effectively and appropriately in a second or foreign language (L2) and to comprehend the L2 even if indirect or conventional expressions are used.* It then asked: *How are intercultural competence and pragmatic competence connected in your view?* Four possible answers and an opt-out option were available to the teachers. There were two preset answers that either established a link between IC and PC—*Pragmatic competence is part of intercultural competence*—or explicitly rejected this—*They are different concepts that are not connected*—along with a *don't know* option and a free-text field in which the teachers could type their own answer if none of the provided ones reflected their views. The responses, given by all 133 participants, are presented in Fig. 6.2.

The results reveal that 86% of the teachers considered pragmatic competence to be part of intercultural competence. The majority, therefore, strongly support the view that pragmaticians have put forward. In addition, 5% of the teachers chose the *don't know* option, and 2% did not think that the two concepts were related. Interestingly, five teachers (4%) wrote the same answer into the free-text field: "intercultural competence is part of pragmatic competence". The other answers provided in the free-text field were:

- "number 2 above [PC is part of IC] to a degree"
- "pragmatic competence is intricately linked to intercultural competence but not subsumed under it, it is more a Venn diagram with a lot of shared space"

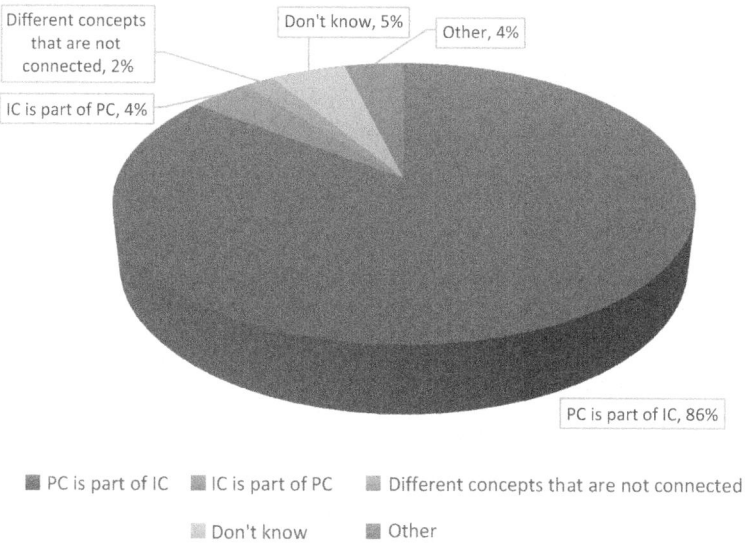

Fig. 6.2 Teachers' views on the relationship between intercultural competence and pragmatic competence (as a percentage of all teachers)

- "is part of communication"
- "related"
- "pragmatic competence is part of intercultural competence but also implies a level of linguistic competence, which may not be incorporated within intercultural competence, although the latter seems a much more complex process"

The individual answers by the teachers thus show that most of them in fact consider intercultural and pragmatic competence to be linked, thereby increasing the overall percentage of teachers who see a link between PC and IC in this study.

To examine if teachers' views differed based on the language they were teaching or thinking of when completing the survey, I also investigated the responses from the 115 members of the seven language groups, which are presented in Table 6.2.

The results reveal that all teachers of four groups (German, French, Dutch and Swedish) consider pragmatic competence to be part of intercultural competence. In the Italian group, all members saw a link between the two, with the clear majority considering PC to be part of IC (90%) and one regarding IC to be part of PC (10%). In the Spanish group, the clear majority again considered PC to be part of IC, with one member choosing the *don't know* option.

The English group was the most diverse with regard to their answers—however, given the considerable differences in the number of teachers in each of the groups and the fact that the English group is the biggest by far, this is not necessarily surprising. As was the case in the other groups, the clear majority of teachers in the English group considered pragmatic

Table 6.2 Teachers' views on the relationship between intercultural competence and pragmatic competence, for each language group

	English	German	Italian	Spanish	French	Dutch	Swedish
PC is part of IC	61 (81%)	11 (100%)	9 (90%)	6 (86%)	6 (100%)	3 (100%)	3 (100%)
IC is part of PC	3 (4%)	0	1 (10%)	0	0	0	0
Unconnected	3 (4%)	0	0	0	0	0	0
Don't know	5 (7%)	0	0	1 (14%)	0	0	0
Other	3 (4%)	0	0	0	0	0	0

competence to be part of intercultural competence (81%). The three English teachers (4%) who are grouped as "other" in Table 6.2 explicitly indicated in their free-text responses that they considered there to be a link but not one that fit the set answers, and the three teachers (4%) who keyed in "IC is part of PC" obviously also saw a link between the two concepts; thus, in fact, a total of 89% of the English teachers considered IC and PC to be linked in some way.

The results of the individual language groups and the MFL teachers as a whole both show that the overwhelming majority of teachers in this study agree that there is a link between the concepts of intercultural competence and pragmatic competence, and this link is seen by teachers working with different languages and in different higher education contexts. This lends support to researchers who have argued that the two concepts are linked and makes the case for overtly establishing a link in teacher training programmes, educational materials and curricula.

6.3 Summary

This chapter presented the results of questions 7a and 7b of the survey, both of which addressed the relationship between intercultural competence and pragmatic competence. Question 7a focused on teachers' familiarity with pragmatic competence. The results revealed that the majority of the teachers, 68%, stated that they were familiar with it, 18% were not familiar with it and 14% chose the *don't know* option. The analysis of the familiarity with pragmatic competence of teachers in each of the seven language groups showed that there were teachers in all groups that stated they were familiar with the term. This is a positive result, as it indicates that there are no L2 teacher communities that are entirely unfamiliar with the term. The percentage scores of the individual groups differed considerably with 86% of the Spanish teachers stating that they were familiar with the term but only 17% of the French teachers reporting the same. However, it needs to be taken into consideration that the group sizes differed and that some groups only consisted of three members. Thus, to obtain more detailed insights into teachers' cognition regarding these terms across different L2s, larger-scale studies are needed.

Question 7b presented the teachers with a definition of pragmatic competence and asked them how pragmatic competence and intercultural competence are linked in their view. The clear majority of the teachers, 86%, considered PC to be part of IC, while 4% regarded IC to be part of

PC. And 2% saw no connection between the two concepts, 5% chose the *don't know* response and the majority of the 4% who answered in other ways also saw a link between IC and PC. The results of the language group analysis revealed that all teachers of four groups (German, French, Dutch and Swedish) considered pragmatic competence to be part of intercultural competence, while the clear majority of the remaining groups (English, Italian and Spanish) did likewise.

The findings of this chapter, therefore, show that the clear majority of the teachers saw a link between intercultural and pragmatic competence. The following chapter focuses on questions around taking account of diversity as part of intercultural competence and addresses teachers' views on gender-neutral language.

References

Bardovi-Harlig, K. (2017). Acquisition of L2 pragmatics. In S. Loewen & M. Sato (Eds.), *The Routledge handbook of instructed second language acquisition* (pp. 224–244). Routledge.

Blum-Kulka, S. (1980). *Learning to say what you mean in a second language: A study of the speech act performance of learners of Hebrew as a second language* [Unpublished manuscript]. https://eric.ed.gov/?id=ED195173

Félix-Brasdefer, J. C. (2018). *Pragmática del español: Contexto, uso y variación*. Routledge.

Finkbeiner, R. (2015). *Einführung in die Pragmatik*. WBG.

Glaser, K. (2018). Enhancing the role of pragmatics in primary English teacher training. *Glottodidactica: An International Journal of Applied Linguistics*, 45(2), 119–131.

House, J. (1982). Opening and closing phrases in German and English dialogues. *Grazer Linguistische Studien*, 16, 52–82.

House, J. (1997). Zum Erwerb interkultureller Kompetenz im Unterricht des Deutschen als Fremdsprache. *Zeitschrift für Interkulturellen Fremdsprachenunterricht*, 1(3), 1–20.

Jackson, J. (2019). Intercultural competence and L2 pragmatics. In N. Taguchi (Ed.), *The Routledge handbook of second language acquisition and pragmatics* (pp. 479–494). Routledge.

Kasper, G. (1981). *Pragmatische Aspekte in der Interrimssprache*. Narr.

Maibauer, J. (2001). *Pragmatik: Eine Einführung*. Stauffenberg.

Maier, A. (2003). Posting the banns: A marriage of pragmatics and culture in foreign and second language pedagogy and beyond. In A. Martínez Flor, E. Usó Juan, & A. Fernández Guerra (Eds.), *Pragmatic competence in foreign language teaching* (pp. 185–210). Publicacions de la Universitat Jaume I.

McConachy, T., & Liddicoat, A. J. (2022). Introduction: Second language pragmatics for intercultural understanding. In T. McConachy & A. J. Liddicoat (Eds.), *Teaching and learning second language pragmatics for intercultural understanding* (pp. 1–18). Routledge.

Nuzzo, E., & Santoro, E. (2017). Apprendimento, insegnamento e uso di competenze pragmatiche in italiano L2/LS: La ricerca a partire dagli anni Duemila. *EuroAmerican Journal of Applied Linguistics and Languages, 4*(2), 1–27.

Olshtain, E., & Cohen, A. D. (1983). Apology: A speech act set. In N. Wolfson & E. Judd (Eds.), *Sociolinguistics and language acquisition* (pp. 18–35). Newbury House.

Placencia, M., & Bravo, D. (2002). *Actos de habla y cortesía en español*. Lincom.

Savvidou, C., & Economidou-Kogetsidis, M. (2019). Teaching pragmatics: Nonnative-speaker teachers' knowledge, beliefs and reported practices. *Intercultural Communication Education, 2*(1), 39–58.

Spencer-Oatey, H. (2010). Intercultural competence and pragmatics research: Examining the interface through studies of intercultural business discourse. In A. Trosborg (Ed.), *Pragmatics across languages and cultures* (pp. 189–218). De Gruyter Mouton.

Taguchi, N., & Roever, C. (2017). *Second language pragmatics*. Oxford University Press.

Usó Juan, E., & Martínez Flor, A. (2021). Teacher pragmatic awareness in English as an international language. In Z. Tajeddin & M. Alemi (Eds.), *Pragmatics pedagogy in English as an international language* (pp. 44–58). Routledge.

Warga, M. (2004). *Pragmatische Entwicklung in der Fremdsprache: Der Sprechakt "Aufforderung" im Französischen*. Gunter Narr.

Open Access This chapter is licensed under the terms of the Creative Commons Attribution 4.0 International License (http://creativecommons.org/licenses/by/4.0/), which permits use, sharing, adaptation, distribution and reproduction in any medium or format, as long as you give appropriate credit to the original author(s) and the source, provide a link to the Creative Commons licence and indicate if changes were made.

The images or other third party material in this chapter are included in the chapter's Creative Commons licence, unless indicated otherwise in a credit line to the material. If material is not included in the chapter's Creative Commons licence and your intended use is not permitted by statutory regulation or exceeds the permitted use, you will need to obtain permission directly from the copyright holder.

CHAPTER 7

Results: Intercultural Competence and Gender-Neutral Language

7.1 TEACHERS' VIEWS ON THE EXISTENCE OF GENDER-NEUTRAL LANGUAGE OPTIONS

In English, there is a long tradition of the use of gender-neutral language (see, e.g., Bodine, 1975) and research on issues related to it (e.g., Bailey et al., 2021; Hyde, 1984; Parks & Roberton, 1998; Rubin & Greene, 1991).[1] Since the 1970s, scholars and organizations have argued for the use of language that does not regard the male as a generic, such as the use of *he* as a generic intended to include individuals of all gender identities (see, e.g., Pauwels, 2003; Nilsen et al., 1977). The use of *they* instead of *he* or *firefighter* instead of *fireman* has now become widely accepted (Freed, 2020). For example, in academic style guides, such as the American Psychological Association's 2020 publication manual, several sections address issues relevant to language, gender and bias, while there are also guidelines for legal professionals on how to use gender-neutral language

---

[1] Other terms that could be used to describe the issue focused on in this chapter include *gender-fair language*, *non-sexist language* and *gender-inclusive language*. The term *gender-neutral language* was chosen in the survey, since it was hoped that this term would be more universally understood than some of the other alternatives, as it is also used by institutions such as the European Parliament (2018). However, it could be the case that misunderstandings arose because of the use of this term over others. Whether this was indeed the case cannot be determined at this point in time, since participants took part anonymously and therefore cannot be contacted. However, it is an issue that future studies may wish to address.

(e.g., Bales, 2002). Discussions about gender-inclusive language started several decades ago in many languages other than English (e.g., German, Spanish, Swedish) as well (see Pauwels, 2003, for early initiatives in several languages; for a recent overview of research, see Formanowicz & Hansen, 2022). However, the acceptance and use of gender-neutral language seems to differ considerably across languages and varieties of languages (e.g., Bonnin & Coronel, 2021; Erdocia, 2022a, b; Kotthoff & Nübling, 2018; Kuhn & Gabriel, 2014; Sarrasin et al., 2012; Vergoossen et al., 2020).

Since the survey was designed for teachers of all modern foreign languages and it was impossible to determine in advance if all languages had gender-neutral forms, question 8a asked teachers about precisely this: *Do gender-neutral expressions or pronouns exist in the L2 you are teaching?* There were four possible preset answer options—*yes, no, don't know* and *no comment*—plus an *other* option, which was a free-text field in which participants could type their individual responses. Figure 7.1 presents the responses to this question.

The question was answered by 132 teachers; one did not respond. Of the remaining 132 teachers, 64% chose *yes*, while 25% selected *no*, 6% chose *don't know* and 5% opted for *other* and then responded with the

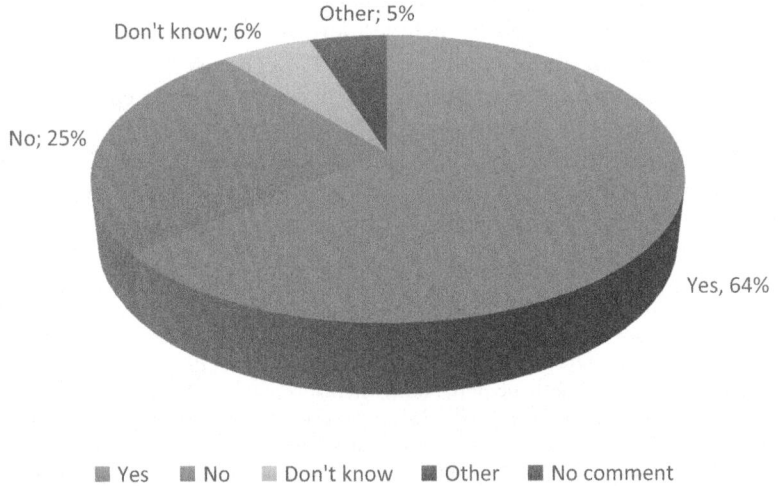

Fig. 7.1 Existence of gender-neutral language options in the L2s they taught, according to the teachers (as a percentage of all teachers who responded)

following in the free-text field (with an indication of the language to which the teacher was referring):

- *Italian*: This discussion is still new
- *English*: Gender-neutral expressions in English are new and a lot of literature in English does not have examples of these expressions
- *English*: Some but there are many that are gender-based
- *Norwegian*: Yes, but it's quite a new phenomenon and only used in specific domains. It has not entered any dictionary, that I know of, yet
- *Dutch*: Not naturally, but there are groups advocating for using certain existing words as gender-neutral pronouns a.t.m.

In addition, there was also a comment about Korean, which unfortunately was phrased ambiguously and has therefore not been included. Since the language the teachers were thinking of is of major importance for this question, the results of the seven language groups (with three or more teachers; see Sect. 3.1) are presented in Table 7.1, and the findings are discussed in relation to the language the teachers were thinking of.

What is highly interesting about the results of this question is that there is no universal agreement with regard to the existence of gender-neutral options in the individual language groups, which I found rather surprising. For example, in Sweden, the gender-neutral pronoun *hen* was introduced as an addition to the existing male (*han*) and female (*hon*) singular pronouns a few years ago. It "is used as both a pronoun to refer to individuals with non-binary gender identities and as a generic pronoun" and "in 2014 the pronoun [*hen*] was included in the Swedish dictionary" (Vergoossen et al., 2020, p. 329). As the introduction of *hen* has continued to receive international media attention over the last few several years (e.g., De Luce, 2019; The Guardian, 2015; Monnis, 2019; Spiegel,

Table 7.1 Existence of gender-neutral language options, according to the teachers of each specific language

	English	*German*	*Italian*	*Spanish*	*French*	*Dutch*	*Swedish*
Yes	60 (80%)	10 (91%)	1 (10%)	3 (43%)	2 (33%)	0	2 (67%)
No	8 (11%)	1 (9%)	8 (80%)	4 (57%)	4 (67%)	2 (67%)	0
Don't know	5 (7%)	0	0	0	0	0	1 (33%)
Other	2 (3%)	0	1 (10%)	0	0	1 (33%)	0

2015), it is puzzling that one of the Swedish teachers selected the *don't know* option. One explanation for the teacher's *don't know* choice could be that she is teaching Swedish in Germany and is thus not as exposed to developments as her two colleagues who are teaching in Sweden. However, even the German language media covered the Swedish pronoun over the years.

Regarding Dutch, one of the teachers mentioned advocacy for gender-neutral language in the free-text field, whereas the others selected *no*. While Gerritsen (2002) reported on developments addressing gender bias in Dutch from the 1970s onward (including the use of plural pronouns instead of male or female singular ones), there do not seem to be recent studies that report on further developments, suggesting that gender-neutral language may not be a widely discussed issue in Dutch.

For the Romance languages, publications address discussions about the issue that have taken place over the last decades, but also highlight the political opposition that some suggestions have encountered (e.g., Erdocia, 2022a, b; Moser et al., 2011; Slemp, 2020; Xiao et al., 2023).

In German, gender-neutral options have been in existence for several years (see, e.g., Diewald & Steinhauer, 2017; Kotthoff & Nübling, 2018) and can be observed in all kinds of institutional discourse settings in the written and spoken language (e.g., higher education, media, politics). Recent initiatives by (far-)right parties to prohibit the use of gender-fair language in public institutions and the media have received considerable attention (Hein, 2023; MDR Online, 2023; Sueddeutsche Zeitung Online, 2023; Zeit Online, 2022; see also Lang, 2017), and it is, therefore, surprising that one of the teachers indicated that gender-neutral language forms do not exist. Like the Swedish teacher who chose *don't know*, the German teachers who selected *no* is also based outside Germany and may not have followed recent developments in Germany from the United States.

The long tradition of gender-neutral language use in English was addressed at the beginning of this chapter. I was, therefore, very surprised that eight teachers indicated that gender-neutral language does not exist in English and that five stated that they did not know about it. Since all teachers who took part in this survey were working in higher education and gender-neutral language forms are a frequent requirement in academic contexts and publications, I was very puzzled by this result. To find out whether these teachers shared any characteristics that may explain their answers, I looked at where they had been working most recently, since the answers from the German and Swedish teacher who had differed from the other group members had suggested that daily exposure to the target language could be a reason.

The analysis of the data showed that all teachers of English who selected either *don't know* or *no* were teaching English in a non-English-speaking country. Another factor that aligned them to the German native speaker who taught Swedish was that 10 of the teachers were non-native speakers of English. This suggests that geographical distance from the target language community and teaching a language that is not one's native language could be factors that lead to less exposure to and awareness of developments in the target language. If this is indeed the case, then teachers working in these circumstances may need to consider expanding their exposure to developments in the L2 more. Higher education institutions, such as language centres, may wish to consider supporting their staff by paying for staff development programmes, newspapers and magazines from the target countries, conferences attendances or educational sojourns in the target L2 context.

Using or not using gender-neutral language can have consequences. As stated above, some professional bodies expect the use of gender-fair, gender-neutral or inclusive language, and in other contexts using or not using gender-neutral language can be seen as a political statement. In addition, individuals addressed with male generic terms who do not identify as male or who object to the use of male generics may be offended by such language directed at them.[2] As my previous research on the perception of L2 learners' language infelicities has shown, native speakers do expect highly proficient L2 learners to use appropriate and inoffensive language and allowances may only be made for L2 learners with a notably low proficiency in the L2 (e.g., Schauer, 2006, 2009). This means that in those languages in which the gender-neutral options have been established, such as English and Swedish, teachers ought to at least be aware of them, so that they can answer their students' questions on this issue and thereby help students make an informed decision on whether or when

---

[2] In German, examples would be the use of *Lehrer* ("teacher"; the word is the singular and plural form for male teachers) for teachers all of genders instead of *Lehrerinnen und Lehrer* (female and male plurals of "teacher") or forms that are inclusive of all genders: *Lehrende, Lehrpersonen, Lehrer:innen* or *Lehrer*innen*.

they need to address gender-neutral options; the teachers' views on this issue are discussed in the following section.

7.2 Teaching Gender-Neutral Language Options or Not

Teachers who had provided an affirmative answer to question 8a were asked to continue on to question 8b: *If gender-neutral language options exist in your L2, do you teach them?* Of the 86[3] teachers who provided an affirmative answer to question 8a, two opted out. The results of the 84 teachers who responded are presented in Fig. 7.2.

The results show that 73% of the teachers taught gender-neutral options, while 18% did not do so, 6% chose not to comment and 4% selected *other* and provided free-text responses as follows:

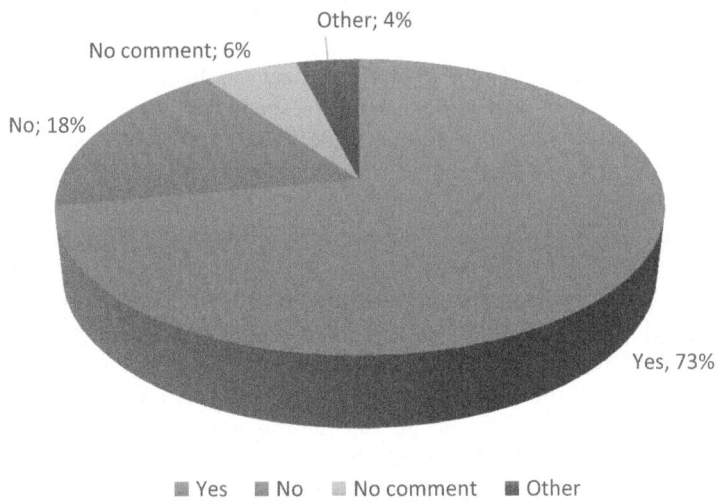

Fig. 7.2 Teaching of gender-neutral language options by the participants (as a percentage of all teachers who responded)

---

[3] The affirmative group consisted of 85 teachers who had answered "yes" and one teacher who had provided an affirmative answer in the free text option (see the Norwegian example in 7.1), thus resulting in 86 teachers in total.

- *English*: Sometimes
- *Spanish*: I mention them and make students aware they do exist but I don't properly teach them
- *French*: I am considering introducing them

To obtain a better understanding of teachers' views, the results for each individual language group were analysed and are presented in Table 7.2. This question was answered by 59 English teachers, nine German teachers, two Italian teachers, three Spanish teachers, two French teachers and two Swedish teachers, thus a total of 77 teachers.

The results show that the majority of English and German teachers who agreed that there were gender-neutral forms in the language they focused on taught gender-neutral language options. Both Italian teachers who had answered question 8a in the affirmative also taught gender-neutral options. In the case of Spanish and French, there was greater variety, with only one Spanish teacher teaching such forms, and the remaining four teachers of Spanish and French either not commenting or providing the free-text comments presented above. Since none of the Dutch teachers provided an affirmative answer to question 8a, they are not represented in Table 7.2. The Swedish teachers that had stated that gender-neutral options existed in Swedish were divided when it came to teaching them, with one doing so and the other not.

I also invited the teachers to share why they did or did not teach gender-neutral forms in their classes in questions 8c and 8d: *If you are (not) teaching gender-neutral language options, you can share your reasons for doing so here*. Fifty-four teachers provided reasons for teaching gender-neutral

Table 7.2 Teaching of gender-neutral language options by the participants in each language group who agreed that there were gender-neutral forms

	English	German	Italian	Spanish	French	Swedish
Yes	42 (71%)	8 (89%)	2 (100%)	1 (33%)		1 (50%)
No	13 (22%)	1 (11%)				1 (50%)
Other	1 (2%)			1 (33%)	1 (50%)	
No comment	3 (5%)			1 (33%)	1 (50%)	

language options in response to question 8c and 15 provided reasons for not teaching gender-neutral language options in response to question 8d. All responses are included in the Appendix to this chapter, in Tables 7.3 and 7.4.

I include here some examples from the data that illustrate why teachers teach gender-neutral language options in different languages[4]:

- *English*: Gender-neutral options are often used in documents and academic contexts, as well as delicate situations, so I believe students should be aware and capable of using them.
- *English*: Firstly, because the use of non-gender-neutral language options in English may hinder understanding and/or communication. Secondly, because it is a matter of culturally appropriate language.
- *English*: Choice of vocabulary is a reflection of one's values. Teaching a language is a lot more than teaching the language. It is teaching another culture as well.
- *English*: They are an important part of knowing the language today and not using them could create problems socially, politically or professionally for my students. More importantly, it is just the right thing to do.
- *English*: My L2 focus is English in which there are grammatically specific situations in which a gender-neutral pronoun is necessary (e.g., "A teacher who works in a school should make enough money. They should never have to worry about pay"). Additionally, I feel it is important that students realize that this isn't just a social issue but grammar as well. I have also implemented a pronoun introduction in the first lessons when we all get to know each other. This I do to try to have an inclusive classroom.
- *English*: Italians have the habit of using the masculine when talking generically. This is not done in English (any more), so I recommend they learn the up-to-date terms like using *they* instead of *he*. This will help them integrate more with their English-speaking counterparts.
- *German*: Using gender-neutral language is a much-discussed topic in Germany. As I see it, it is part of a development towards inclusion and acceptance of minorities and therefore something students in a

---

[4] The comments have occasionally been modified slightly here to address typos, etc. The original comments can be found in the Appendix.

language class should deal with. It is part of the acquisition of intercultural competence.
- *Italian*: I usually try to make students aware of the options they have and what political implications each option entails. Then, it is up to them to make their own language choices so as to convey their intentions and project the image they want to project in specific contexts. I don't really insist too much on this topic for now, because the discussion is still very much open in Italian and even native speakers who choose to adopt an inclusive language are often criticized for that.
- *Spanish*: Pragmatic relevance.
- *French*: I think it is important to make students aware of the variety of pronouns that exist but also make them aware that they may not be accepted or even understood by all (e.g., *iel* in French). It can also help non-binary, genderqueer, gender-fluid students to express their identity in the target language.
- *Swedish*: Because it is part of the language.

The examples provided represent the breadth of reasons given for teaching gender-neutral language. I coded the responses by the teachers who had answered this question according to themes and found that the following could be identified in the data: inclusion (9 responses), equality (7), everyday language use (6), to address negative transfer from the L1 (5), to avoid offence (5), academic language conventions (4), culture (4), grammar (3), (in)appropriate language (3), part of language (3) and values (2).[5] In addition, teachers also referred to diversityLGBTIQA aspects such as the community and non-binary individuals, thus also linking gender-neutral language to gender identity. The examples illustrate the variety of reasons offered by the teachers and also show the link between gender-neutral language options, intercultural competence and pragmatics.

Fifteen teachers responded to question 8d and commented on why they were not teaching gender-neutral language. Comments illustrating some of the reasons given are:

---

[5] Other codes and code combinations are, of course, possible. The complete responses from the teachers are provided in the Appendix to this chapter so that readers can access them and follow common themes.

- *English*: There are only very few and they come along automatically when dealing with different topics. So, it is not necessary to make them an explicitly addressed topic in class.
- *English*: I teach C1+ and at this level the students are probably more aware of this than I am—internet, YouTube, TikTok, etc.
- *English*: I teach [English for Specific Purposes] at a science faculty. Based on the topics I have been teaching, I have not felt the need to address this particular issue in my classes so far.
- *English*: In my 20+ years of teaching, I've always used *he or she*.
- *German*: I don't agree with it.
- *Italian*: I teach Italian. There are very few and unimportant gender-neutral forms.

What is interesting about the comments is that only few of them show opposition towards gender-neutral language (e.g., the responses by the German teacher given above). Instead, the themes that emerge in this data set tend to indicate that the learners are already aware of them (see the comment by an English teacher above), that gender-neutral options are featured in materials the students are exposed to (in two comments) or that teachers talk about them in class to raise awareness but do not consider that to be teaching them (in three comments). In addition, there are variations on the theme of gender-neutral language not being particularly relevant or even being distracting (in four comments). One teacher commented on a political stance that is not shared by the learners, while another indicated that they would like to pay more attention to it; and one (included above) refers to explicitly always using gender-binary forms. The responses by the teachers underline the importance of conducting research that gives participants the opportunity to voice their own thoughts, especially when issues that could be perceived as delicate or political as in the case of gender-neutral language are examined. If teachers had not been given the opportunity in this survey to explain why they teach or do not teach gender-neutral language, it would have been easy to make assumptions about their responses to question 8b that could then have been instrumentalized.[6]

---

[6] Obtaining information on why participants choose specific options offered in a questionnaire is something that I believe we ought to focus on more, as it will enable us to better understand informants' opinions and thought processes, especially if their answers differ from our own as researchers. Combining quantitative and qualitative elements in data collection may not always be possible, but it has the potential to offer a much more intricate picture of why people think the way they do (see, e.g., Schauer, 2006, 2009, 2017, for combined qualitative and quantitative approaches in pragmatics).

It is also important to bear in mind that the teachers in this study represent a variety of different languages. While not using gender-neutral language options in certain contexts and languages may be considered marked or offensive, or as making a political statement, using gender-neutral options in languages in which they are not as established could also be regarded as taking a certain political stance. My personal view has always been that language educators should make their students aware of developments affecting language and the impact that particular language choices can have. Unless laid down in university regulations, it is then up to the students to decide how they wish to express themselves and to live with the consequences. However, in order to make informed decisions, students need precisely that—information. If educators want their learners to become successful intercultural communicators and to be able to communicate effectively and appropriately, they need to provide them with information that will allow them to do so.

7.3 Summary

This chapter presented the analysis of the responses to questions 8a–8d, which focused on gender-neutral language. Question 8a explored whether gender-neutral language options existed in the L2s taught by the teachers, in their opinion. The results revealed that 64% of the teachers stated that the L2 they taught offered these options, while 25% answered that this was not the case. In addition, 6% of the teachers chose *don't know* and 5% opted for the *other* option, providing their comments in a free-text field. The analysis of the seven language groups showed that teachers in the individual groups tended to have different views on the existence of gender-neutral language options in their respective language, which was a surprising result.

The teachers who answered question 8a in the affirmative were then asked whether they taught gender-neutral options or not (question 8b) and to explain why they did (question 8c) or did not do so (question 8d). The answers to question 8b showed that 73% of this subset of teachers taught gender-neutral options, while 18% did not do so. The answers also showed that 6% chose not to comment and 4% selected the *other* option. Teachers provided a variety of reasons for why they taught gender-neutral options, with the most frequently mentioned themes being inclusion, equality, gender-neutral language being part of everyday language use, avoiding negative transfer from learners' L1, academic language conventions and it being part of the target language's culture. The responses from the teachers who taught gender-neutral language options indicated that they considered gender-neutral language to be linked to intercultural communicative competence and pragmatics.

The responses of the teachers who did not teach gender-neutral language revealed that a third of them did not do so because they either talked about them in class but did not consider that to be outright teaching, or because gender-neutral options were covered in the materials anyway. Other teachers indicated that these options were not relevant in the respective language or were too distracting for their learners. Two teachers stated that they did not teach them because they disagreed with them, while others were interested in using them or referred to using explicit binary language options.

Overall, the data showed that gender-neutral language is an area worthy of further discussion in studies that address the interface between pragmatics and intercultural communicative competence.

Appendix

Table 7.3 Teachers' reasons for teaching gender-neutral language (by language taught)

Question 8c	
Language	Comment
English	Know how to use gender-neutral language is part, or should be, of everyday language usage.
English	So students are aware of impact of language choice
English	Students need to respect values (even if only being discussed) present in the L2.
English	Because gender-neutral pronouns are fast becoming common/accepted usage and because feminism

(continued)

Table 7.3 (continued)

Question 8c

Language	Comment
English	I feel students need to be made aware that language and gender (in)equality are connected.
English	Gender-neutral expressions are more inclusive.
English	Extension of grammar class (everyone-> they), knowledge of current issues, reference to debates in French (L1), material taken from Kae Tempest who uses "they".
English	Gender-neutral pronouns are often used in academic English and press, and it is important for students to know how to use them properly when referring to their colleagues and instructors.
English	In a world that should embrace all genders and sexual orientations it is mandatory to teach others how to address people in order to prevent feelings of disappointment, inferiority, discomfort or even insult.
English	For reasons of both style and inclusivity.
English	I'm teaching English mostly to L1 German speakers. To my view, the German language has many more gender-neutral language options than English, that's why, very often in the class, students simply ask—why it is so and no so?; the most recent example I have- in the beginning of the class I said: "Hello, guys". One of the student got confused and said: "Isn't guys a word you would address to male only?". Technically, she is right, but we still use it in English when addressing to the group of people consisting of guys and girls; so I started paying more attention to the words like actor-actress, waiter-waitress, flight-attendant, etc. when teaching.
English	To make the learner aware of it, esp. if this is not the case in L1
English	Not only because these options are politically correct, but because native speakers are sensitive to their use.
English	Why wouldn't I? Gender-neutral language is an integral part of the English language. In fact, it is necessary to go beyond gender-neutral language and include inclusive language that does not discriminate against other groups, including persons with disabilities, older people, LGBTQ+ groups, etc.
English	Students often misuse pronouns because their L1 might dictate that. For example, Italian has "il suo viso" for "his face", but you could also be talking about a woman. I find that students need to be aware of the L1/L2 difference and then will make appropriate gender-neutral choices, too.
English	I would say there is generally wide acceptance of gender-neutral language in English-speaking countries. This is accompanied by an increased sensitivity and awareness of the necessity to teach this in English language classrooms. This is why I teach it.
English	For reasons of inclusivity
English	It is the property of the L2 I teach, so it must be taught.

(*continued*)

Table 7.3 (continued)

Question 8c	
Language	Comment
English	Gender-neutral options are often used in documents and academic contexts, as well as delicate situations, so I believe students should be aware and capable of using them.
English	(1) to raise awareness of gender issues; (2) to help student write/speak in a way that will be least likely to cause offense
English	In English it is quite natural to use these options.
English	Part of everyday life, part of the host culture
English	Firstly, because the use of non-gender-neutral language options in English may hinder understanding and/or communication. Secondly, because it is a matter of culturally appropriate language.
English	To raise awareness of gender equality. E.g. instead of students talking about 'his essay' when using an exemplar, I would teach "their".
English	Equitable treatment of all individuals.;; singular "they" in English for unspecified gender is useful because:;—it is easy to remember;;—it has already been in use for unspecified persons for a long time;;—it prevents the purely cognitive problems that would arise were there to be 12 different pronouns to remember.
English	I try to teach gender neuter language through my classroom discourse and materials I make. I think this is important because there can be a natural bias towards always using the gender of oneself as the default option (probably especially true for males, which I am). It was actually pointed out to me early in my career that I had a tendency to do this; that has stuck with me and I've made an effort to reflect gender equality in my teaching language ever since.
English	Required to achieve academic style and maintain anonymity
English	I teach the English "they" for third person singular, gender-neutral, because it's very useful for formal purposes in academic writing or when you don't know the gender. I often also take the opportunity to raise its use outside academia for people whose gender identity is not binary.
English	When I receive questions from my students, then I will
English	They are an important part of knowing the language today and not using them could create problems socially, politically, or professionally for my students. More importantly, it is just the right thing to do.
English	I teach academic English, so they are necessary.
English	Choice of vocabulary is a reflection of ones values. Teaching a language is a lot more than teaching the language. It is teaching another culture as well.
English	I always give the "original" terms followed by the updated gender-neutral term. For example, I would say that you can say a policeman or a policewoman, but that you can use police officer to refer to all. Same with terms such as firefighter.

(*continued*)

Table 7.3 (continued)

Question 8c

Language	Comment
English	Italians have the habit of using the masculine when talking generically. This is not done in English (any more), so I recommend they learn the uptodate terms like using "they" instead of "he". This will help them integrate more with their English speaking counterparts.
English	Teaching French students English, they often use "his" or "him" as they translate it directly from French: "son" or "lui". I remind them that not all *insert group of people here* are male, and that they can use "they" or "their" to avoid referring to just one gender.
English	Gender-neutral language is necessary in many contexts.
English	Equality requirement of university
English	My L2 focus is English in which there are grammatically specific situations in which a gender-neutral pronoun is necessary (e.g., "A teacher who works in a school should make enough money. They should never have to worry about pay"). Additionally, I feel it is important that students realize that this isn't just a social issue, but grammar as well. I have also implemented a pronoun introduction in the first lessons when we all get to know each other. This I do to try to have an inclusive classroom.
English	This is a very hot topic in the US, which has shown ever-increasing sensitivity to gender bias. My goal is not to necessarily hammer the usage of gender-neutral language into my students' speech or writing, but it is to make them aware that this is a touchy subject in some societies. This is absolutely something that many German learners are unaware of until they start B1/B2 level courses, where they start writing more complex letters, essays, etc. (especially, if it's a "Business English" course of any kind). If I can make them aware of such sensitivity, as well as nuances for improvement, I at least feel as if I've done my job.
English	[My] University prides itself to be an inclusive institution. We do have a number of non-binary students and in the second final year in particular are expressively discussing the role of sex, gender and identity both in our cultural and our language modules
English	To inform the learner and make them aware of the fact.
German	In the case of German it is an absolute necessity to explain to students gender-neutral language options, as the students can get into trouble if they use inappropriate terms
German	I am not really sure, but I teach the male and female forms of professions and create awareness with the students. I have learned about first steps to gender-neutral pronouns in my language just this year. They look and feel very unnatural to me at the moment but I intend to do a training this month and plan to present the forms to my students next academic year. I hope this will trigger some interesting discussions.

(*continued*)

Table 7.3 (continued)

Question 8c

Language	Comment
German	égalité
German	Ich bin mir nicht sicher, ob ich richtig verstanden habe… ich versuche, meine Studierenden für die genderdifferenzierenden Formen zu sensibilisieren und verwende sie selber (Binnen-I / Sternchen, Passiv-Umschreibungen, etc) ["I am not sure if I understood the question correctly… I try to make my students more sensitive towards gender differentiating forms and also use them myself (*various options for gender-neutral language mentioned*)"]
German	Gender equality and cultural competence
German	Using gender-neutral language is a much discussed topic in Germany. As I see it, it is part of a development towards inclusion and acceptance of minorities and therefore something students in a language class should deal with. It is part of the acquisition of intercultural competence.
Italian	I teach a Romance language which has a rigid binary grammar. Inclusive language is a unique way to focus on grammar in a more relevant way
Italian	I usually try to make students aware of the options they have and what political implications each option entails. Then, it is up to them to make their own language choices so as to convey their intentions and project the image they want to project in specific contexts. I don't really insist too much on this topic for now, because the discussion is still very much open in Italian and even native speakers who choose to adopt an inclusive language are often criticised for that...
Spanish	Pragmatic relevance
French	I think it is important to make students aware of the variety of pronouns that exist, but also make them aware that they may not be accepted or even understood by all (e.g., iel in French). It can also help non-binary, gender queer, genderfluid students to express their identity in the target language.
Swedish	Because it is part of the language
Korean	If Korean had many gender-neutral terms I would teach them. Korea is conservative and although there are gendered issues in the language that relate to how one addresses others (esp. brother/sister words) there has been on clear movement in Korea to address these as far as I am aware and I have checked this.
Norwegian	I mention and explain it to be a form/word that can be found/read/heard sometimes in everyday language, especially the press and social media and that it has been a development in the last couple of years, adapted from another language. Also, I teach that it's not part of dictionaries etc. yet and that there are both people in favour and against the language development. My main reason for teaching gender-neutral language options is for the students to recognize the words in texts, give them the possibility to adapt their own language use and to show how the L2 is evolving (as we speak).

Table 7.4 Teachers' reasons for *not* teaching gender-neutral language (by language taught)

Question 8d

Language	Comment
English	Basically, it is concept triage. Gender-neutral forms will be encountered less often than other material my students need for their level/purposes
English	It is already foregrounded as an absolute in the studied texts and not an aspect to be singled out and taught specially.
English	They signal an explicit political position, one which may not be shared by learners.
English	There are only very few and they come along automatically when dealing with different topics. So it is not necessary to make them an explicitly addressed topic in class.
English	I teach ESP at a science faculty. Based on the topics I have been teaching, I have not felt the need to address this particular issue in my classes so far.
English	I talk about it in class but don't specifically teach it; probably because it doesn't appear in course material and is not part of the curriculum.
English	I don't consciously pick out gender-neutral language for teaching although I do try to use it inside and outside the classroom. I just try to make students aware of the options and what they mean [or is that teaching gender-neutral language?]
English	Probably not cautious enough about neutral gender forms! However, I would like to pay more attention to it!
English	In my +20 years of teaching, I've always used "he or she".
English	I teach C1 + and at this level the students are probably more aware of this than I am—internet, YouTube, TikTok etc.
English	I may teach gender-neutral pronouns later when their use becomes more widespread. For now, I think it teaching them would be introducing an unnecessary distraction.
English	It generally comes up naturally when we are having discussions in class but is not something that I feel is particularly important to teach explicitly or to plan into my materials.
German	I don't agree with it
Italian	I teach Italian. There are very few and unimportant gender-neutral forms.
Swedish	Since the neutral pronoun use has been established after I left my homecountry I dont une it personnaly so I dont teach it. I also have a difficulty to accept these using and its purpose. I also find it as a supplementary difficulty because the sutdents already dont une the feminin and masculin pronouns properly.

References

American Psychological Association. (2020). *Publication manual: The official guide to APA style* (7th ed.). American Psychological Association.

Bailey, A. H., Dovidio, J. F., & LaFrance, M. (2021). "Master" of none: Institutional language change linked to reduced gender bias. *Journal of Experimental Psychology: Applied, 28*(1), 237–248.

Bales, R. A. (2002). Gender-neutral language. *Bench & Bar Kentucky, 66*(3), 40–41.

Bodine, A. (1975). Androcentrism in prescriptive grammar: Singular "they", sex-indefinite "he", and "he or she". *Language in Society, 4,* 129–146.

Bonnin, J. E., & Coronel, A. A. (2021). Attitudes toward gender-neutral Spanish: Acceptability and adoptability. *Frontiers in Sociology, 6.* https://doi.org/10.3389/fsoc.2021.629616

De Luce, I. (2019, August 19). Sweden recently introduced a gender-neutral pronoun: Psychologists say it's already changing the way people think. *Business Insider.* https://www.businessinsider.com/sweden-has-non-gendered-pronoun-changing-the-way-people-think-2019-8

Diewald, G., & Steinhauer, A. (2017). *Richtig gendern: Wie Sie angemessen und verständlich schreiben.* Duden Verlag.

Erdocia, I. (2022a). Language and culture wars: The far right's struggle against gender-neutral language. *Journal of Language and Politics, 21*(6), 847–866.

Erdocia, I. (2022b). Participation and deliberation in language policy: The case of gender-neutral language. *Current Issues in Language Planning, 23*(4), 435–455.

European Parliament. (2018). *Gender-neutral language in the European Parliament.* https://www.europarl.europa.eu/cmsdata/151780/GNL_Guidelines_EN.pdf

Formanowicz, M., & Hansen, K. (2022). Subtle linguistic cues affecting gender in(equality). *Journal of Language and Social Psychology, 41*(2), 127–147.

Freed, A. F. (2020). Women, language and public discourse: Five decades of sexism and scrutiny. In C. R. Caldas-Coulthard (Ed.), *Innovations and challenges: Women, language and sexism* (pp. 3–18). Routledge.

Gerritsen, M. (2002). Language and gender in Netherlands Dutch: Towards a more gender-fair usage. In M. Hellinger & H. Bußmann (Eds.), *Gender across languages* (pp. 81–108). John Benjamins.

Hein, D. (2023, March 24). *Dresdner Stadtrat beschließt Anti-Gender-Regeln.* Sächsische.de. https://www.saechsische.de/dresden/politik/dresdner-stadtrat-beschliesst-anti-gender-regeln-5837931.html.

Hyde, J. S. (1984). Children's understanding of sexist language. *Developmental Psychology, 20*(4), 697–706.

Kotthoff, H., & Nübling, D. (2018). *Genderlinguistik: Eine Einführung in Sprache, Gespräch und Geschlecht.* Narr.

Kuhn, E. A., & Gabriel, U. (2014). Actual and potential gender-fair language use: The role of language competence and the motivation to use accurate language. *Journal of Language and Social Psychology, 33*(2), 214–225.

Lang, J. (2017, November 20). *"Gender" und "Genderwahn": Neue Feindbilder der extremen Rechten.* Bundeszentrale für Politische Bildung. https://www.bpb.de/themen/rechtsextremismus/dossier-rechtsextremismus/259953/gender-und-genderwahn-neue-feindbilder-der-extremen-rechten/

MDR Online. (2023, February 10). *Schmalkalden-Meiningen: AfD-Kreistagsfraktion scheitert mit Antrag gegen das Gendern.* MDR Online. https://www.mdr.de/nachrichten/thueringen/sued-thueringen/schmalkalden-meiningen/afd-gendern-verwaltung-kreistag-100.html

Monnis, M. (2019, August 18). *"Le parole sono importanti" e i pronomi neutri possono davvero ridurre i pregiudizi di genere.* Elle Italia Online https://www.elle.com/it/magazine/women-in-society/a28658706/pronomi-neutri-quali-sono/

Moser, F., Sato, S., Chiarini, T., Dmitrow-Devold, K., & Kuhn, E. (2011). *Comparative analysis of existing guidelines for gender-fair language within the ITN LCG Network—Work package B: Report on milestone 1.* Marie Curie Initial Training Network.

Nilsen, A. P., Bosmajian, H., Gershuny, H. L., & Stanley, J. P. (1977). *Sexism and language.* National Council of Teachers of English.

Parks, J. B., & Roberton, M. A. (1998). Contemporary arguments against non-sexist language: Blaubergs (1980) revisited. *Sex Roles, 39*(5/6), 445–461.

Pauwels, A. (2003). Linguistic sexism and feminist linguistic activism. In J. Holmes & M. Meyerhoff (Eds.), *The handbook of language and gender* (pp. 550–570). Wiley.

Rubin, D. L., & Greene, K. L. (1991). Effects of biological and psychological gender, age cohort, and interviewer gender on attitudes toward gender-inclusive/exclusive language. *Sex Roles, 24*(7–8), 391–411.

Sarrasin, O., Gabriel, U., & Gygax, P. (2012). Sexism and attitudes toward gender-neutral language: The case of English, French, and German. *Swiss Journal of Psychology, 71*(3), 113–124.

Schauer, G. A. (2006). Pragmatic awareness in ESL and EFL contexts: Contrast and development. *Language Learning, 56*(2), 269–318.

Schauer, G. A. (2009). Interlanguage pragmatic development: The study abroad context. *Continuum.*

Schauer, G. A. (2017). "It's really insulting to say something like that to anyone": An investigation of English and German native speakers' impoliteness perceptions. In I. Kecskes & S. Assimakopoulos (Eds.), *Current issues in intercultural pragmatics* (pp. 207–227). John Benjamins.

Slemp, K. (2020). *Latino, Latina, Latin@, Latine, and Latinx: Gender inclusive oral expression in Spanish* [Master's thesis, University of Western Ontario]. Electronic Thesis and Dissertation Repository. https://ir.lib.uwo.ca/etd/7297

Spiegel. (2015, March 25). *Schwedische Sprache: Nicht Mann, nicht Frau, sondern "hen"*. Spiegel Online. https://www.spiegel.de/lebenundlernen/schule/schule-schweden-neues-geschlechtsneutrales-personalpronomen-a-1025479.html

Sueddeutsche Zeitung Online. (2023, February 2). *Kontroverse Debatte über Gendersprache in der Bürgerschaft*. SZ Online. https://www.sueddeutsche.de/politik/buergerschaft-hamburg-kontroverse-debatte-ueber-gendersprache-in-der-buergerschaft-dpa.urn-newsml-dpa-com-20090101-230131-99-427812

The Guardian. (2015, March 24). *Sweden adds gender-neutral pronoun to dictionary*. Guardian Online. https://www.theguardian.com/world/2015/mar/24/sweden-adds-gender-neutral-pronoun-to-dictionary.

Vergoossen, H. P., Renström, E. A., Lindqvist, A., & Gustafsson Sendén, M. (2020). Four dimensions of criticism against gender-fair language. *Sex Roles, 83*, 328–337.

Xiao, H., Strickland, B., & Peperkamp, S. (2023). How fair is gender-fair language? Insights from gender ratio estimations in French. *Journal of Language and Social Psychology, 42*(1), 82–106.

Zeit Online. (2022, November 11). *Thüringer Landtag stimmt für Antigenderantrag*. Zeit Online. https://www.zeit.de/politik/deutschland/2022-11/gendern-thueringen-landtag-abstimmung-afd-linke-ablehnung.

Open Access This chapter is licensed under the terms of the Creative Commons Attribution 4.0 International License (http://creativecommons.org/licenses/by/4.0/), which permits use, sharing, adaptation, distribution and reproduction in any medium or format, as long as you give appropriate credit to the original author(s) and the source, provide a link to the Creative Commons licence and indicate if changes were made.

The images or other third party material in this chapter are included in the chapter's Creative Commons licence, unless indicated otherwise in a credit line to the material. If material is not included in the chapter's Creative Commons licence and your intended use is not permitted by statutory regulation or exceeds the permitted use, you will need to obtain permission directly from the copyright holder.

CHAPTER 8

Results: Intercultural Competence in Modern Foreign Language Teacher Education

8.1 Coverage of Intercultural Competence in Higher Education

This chapter focuses on the MFL teachers' own educational background. As Kelly (2020, p. 330) writes in his handbook chapter on intercultural second language teacher education, "a growing number of countries include aspects of intercultural or sociocultural pedagogy in the training of teachers". Since the first edition of Byram's monograph *Teaching and assessing intercultural communicative competence*, which had a considerable impact on the EU educational policy, was published in 1997, several international bodies have published policy papers highlighting the importance of intercultural education (e.g., CoE, 2014; UNESCO, 2013), frequently referring to Byram's ICC model. It is, therefore, only to be expected that higher educational institutions in the EU but also worldwide (e.g., Fantini, 2020; Moloney et al., 2020; Savignon & Sysoyev, 2005) would try to provide their students with information on ICC in their modern foreign language teacher training programmes. While I encountered intercultural communicative competence and Byram's framework in a seminar offered by Zoltan Dörnyei in the early 2000s, not all modern foreign language teachers would have been so fortunate to learn about the concepts so soon after Byram's 1997 monograph or Fantini's well-known 1995 article were published. Indeed, as some MFL teachers completed their higher educational studies prior to the appearance of these and other publications on the subject, they would not have been able to encounter ICC when they were studying for their degrees.

In developing this research project, I very much hoped that the survey would be completed by a highly diverse group of teachers representing different modern foreign languages, years of teaching experience, genders and ages. Because of this, I felt it important to also ask the teachers if they had encountered intercultural competence during their own higher education studies. Figure 8.1 presents the teachers' responses to question 9a: *Was intercultural competence addressed during your university studies?*

This question was answered by 132 participants. The results show that the percentage of teachers who responded that they did and did not encounter intercultural competence during their higher education studies is nearly even, with 48% not encountering it and 44% encountering it. In addition, 8% of the teachers chose *don't know* and 1% preferred not to comment. As discussed in the methodology and in the first four chapters reporting results, the sample of teachers who participated in this research is rather diverse with regard to several characteristics. While in the discussion thus far I have mainly focused on the different languages taught by the teachers—and will do likewise in this chapter—for questions 9a and 9b it is also interesting to analyse the data taking account of the teachers' ages. While it is, of course, possible to attend university later in life, and

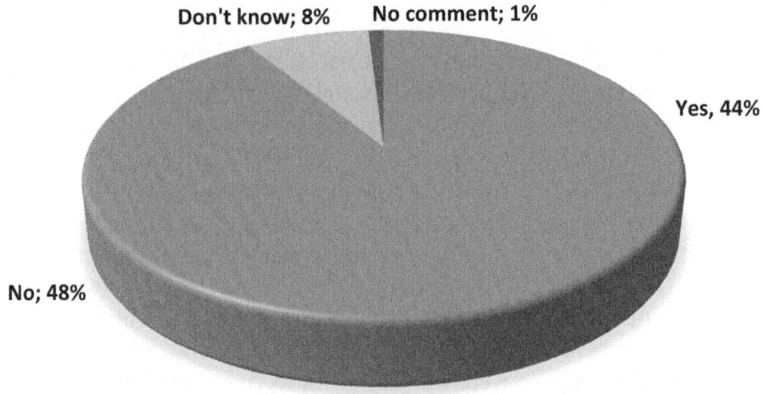

Fig. 8.1 Coverage of intercultural competence in their higher education studies according to the participants (as a percentage of total responses)

Table 8.1 Coverage of intercultural competence in their higher education according to the participants, for each age group

Age group	Teachers who responded yes		Teachers who responded no		Teachers who responded don't know	
	Number	% of age group	Number	% of age group	Number	% of age group
20–29	7	64%	2	18%	2	18%
30–39	20	65%	6	19%	5	16%
40–49	13	37%	21	60%	1	3%
50–59	12	33%	23	64%	1	3%
60+	5	29%	11	65%	1	6%

thus there may not always be a direct link between one's age and the time when one attended a particular education institution, the data here show that those participants in the higher age ranges normally had more years of teaching experience, thus pointing to most of them having completed their studies several years ago.[1]

The analysis of the encounters of the teachers with IC during their higher education studies based on age group is presented in Table 8.1. As set out in Chap. 3, teachers could choose one of five different age groups or decide to opt out of this question. Of the 132 teachers who answered question 9a, 130 provided information regarding their age. The age groups were as follows: 20–29 years (11 teachers), 30–39 years (31 teachers), 40–49 years (35 teachers), 50–59 years (36 teachers) and 60+ years (17 teachers).

The results show that—as had been anticipated—there is an inverse relationship between age and coverage of IC during higher education studies. In the younger teacher groups (i.e., those aged 20–39), the majority of the teachers encountered IC during their higher education studies, while in the older age groups (40–60+), the majority of teachers did not. This notable difference is schematically illustrated in Fig. 8.2.

---

[1] Many of the personal background questions are based on Sercu et al. (2005) or are slight modifications of the questions asked in their study. Future studies may consider adding background questions that provide more precise information on when teachers completed their degrees. I decided against asking precise questions in this study as I worried that teachers may not wish to answer them in order to protect their anonymity, as being asked to provide a substantial amount of personal background information may deter participants from taking part or completing the questionnaire.

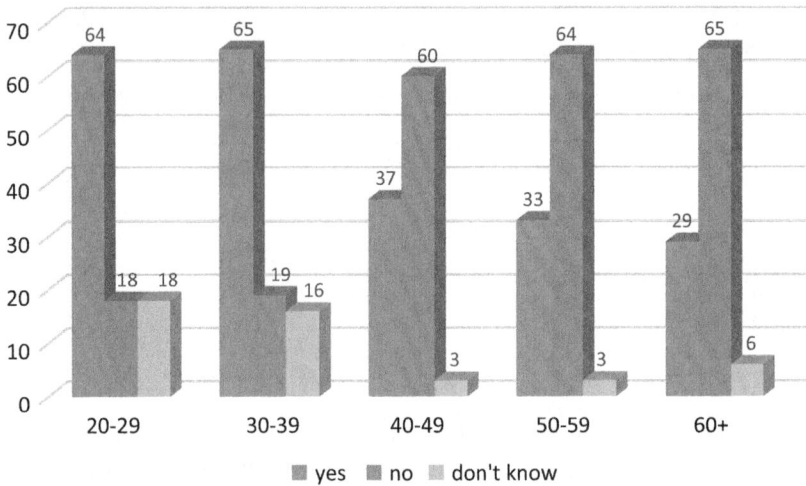

Fig. 8.2 Coverage of intercultural competence in their higher education according to the participants, by age group

The findings also indicate that higher educational institutions currently offering teacher training programmes may wish to consider to what extent—if at all—they address intercultural (communicative) competence in their programmes, since not all of the newly or relatively recently qualified teachers had encountered the concepts, based on this self-report data. Higher educational institutions involved in MFL teaching ought to consider supporting professional development initiatives that provide their staff with the opportunity to obtain information on issues that perhaps may not have been addressed during their own teacher training, as also mentioned in Chap. 7.

In addition to analysing the responses to question 9a based on age groups, I also examined the data in terms of the language groups, as presented in Table 8.2.

The data do not indicate any clear link between the L2 taught and teachers having encountered IC during their own studies in the case of English, German, Italian and French. In the Spanish group, the majority stated that IC was not covered, and the same is true for the Dutch and Swedish groups; but group size must be taken into consideration.

Table 8.2 Coverage of intercultural competence in their higher education according to the participants, for each language group

	English	German	Italian	Spanish	French	Dutch	Swedish
Yes	33 (44%)	7 (64%)	5 (50%)	1 (14%)	3 (50%)	1 (33%)	0
No	35 (47%)	4 (36%)	4 (40%)	5 (71%)	3 (50%)	2 (67%)	2 (67%)
Don't know	7 (9%)	0	1 (10%)	1 (14%)	0	0	1 (33%)
No comment	0	0	0	0	0	0	0

8.2 SCHOLARS ASSOCIATED WITH INTERCULTURAL COMPETENCE

In addition to finding out whether IC had been covered during the participants' own higher educational studies, I was interested in learning more about the scholars that the teachers associated with IC and therefore asked them in 9b: *Do you associate particular scholars with intercultural competence?* The names of five IC researchers had been included as possible answer options—Michael Byram, Alvino Fantini, Sandra Savignon, Helen Spencer-Oatey and Stella Ting-Toomey—but participants were invited to add as many others as they liked.

This question was only answered by 51 participants, fewer than half of the participants that took part in the survey, which presumably indicates that the majority of the teachers did not link the names of particular scholars to IC. Since 58 teachers had stated that they encountered IC during their higher education in response to question 9a, it could be assumed that 51 of them then selected familiar names or typed in the names of scholars they had encountered during their own studies.

However, this is not the case. Instead, the picture is more mixed, with teachers who had not encountered IC during their studies providing or selecting names, and others not doing so even though they had learned about it during their own higher education studies. This also suggests that at least some of the teachers who did not encounter IC during their own studies—or could not remember doing so and therefore chose the *don't know* option—had learned about it in some other way, perhaps while doing independent reading, in formal in-service teacher education development programmes or in more informal settings (e.g., chats with fellow

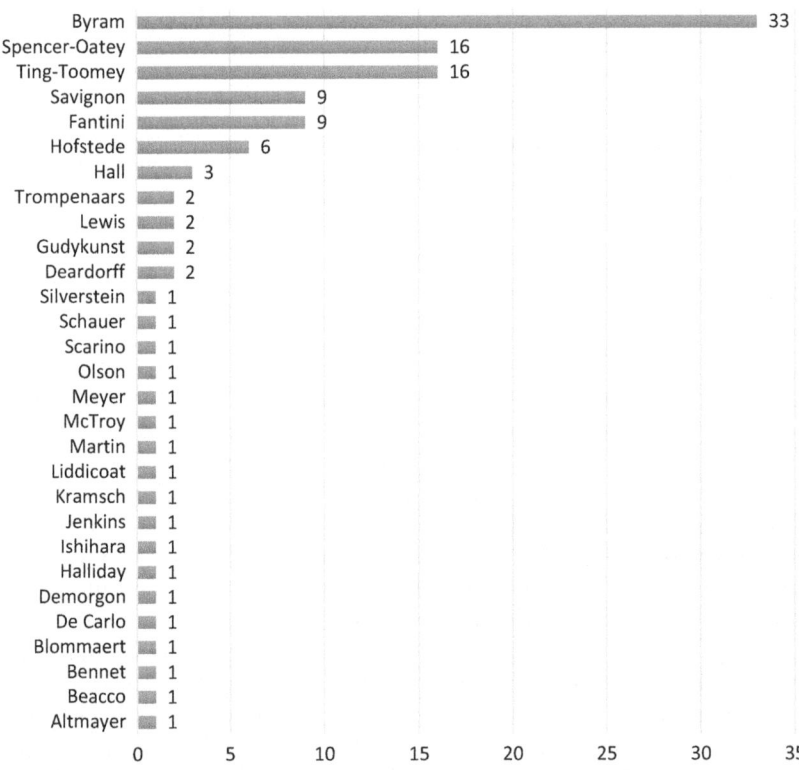

Fig. 8.3 Scholars whom participants associated with IC, ordered by the number of teachers who mentioned them

teachers). The overview of all scholars mentioned by the teachers who answered this question is provided in Fig. 8.3.[2]

The results are presented here in terms of the number of teachers (rather than a percentage), since there were many scholars that were named only by a single teacher. The results show that the majority, 65% of the teachers, associated Michael Byram with IC followed by Helen Spencer-Oatey and Stella Ting-Toomey (both with 31%), Alvino Fantini and Sandra Savignon (both with 18%) and Geert Hofstede (12%). All

---

[2] Teachers could choose as many names as they wished and could also add as many names as they wished.

other scholars were named by fewer than 10% of the teachers who responded to this question. Thus, the results indicate that L2 teachers working in higher education who are familiar with IC also tend to be familiar with very well-known scholars in the field while also showing awareness of a wider variety of scholars researching IC.

I was also interested in exploring if teachers' knowledge of scholars associated with IC was connected to the language that the teachers taught and therefore analysed the data accordingly. The results are presented in Table 8.3 and reflect the data from 29 English teachers, six German teachers, four Italian teachers, three Spanish teachers, two French teachers and one Swedish teacher (a total of 45 teachers).

The findings show that the majority of the scholars who were associated with IC by more than 10% of the teachers who answered this question were also named by teachers representing different languages. For example, Byram was named by teachers from all language groups but the Dutch one (though it is important to take into consideration that the Dutch group consisted of only three members, none of whom named anyone in this question). A striking finding is, however, that Hofstede was only named by English teachers. Based on the data, it is not clear why this occurred, since the data revealed no other factor that could explain this, as the teachers who added his name had studied and worked in a variety of different countries and shared no other background features explored in the survey. Overall, it would be interesting to have more research on names associated with IC from a variety of MFL groups, as this may provide insights into the models and conceptualizations of IC that teachers have encountered during their training and career and which may be informing their own teaching. Data from different parts of the world would be particularly interesting in this light.

Table 8.3 Scholars whom participants in each language group associated with intercultural competence

	English	German	Italian	Spanish	French	Dutch	Swedish	**Total**
Byram	15	6	4	2	2	0	1	**30**
Fantini	7	1	0	0	0	0	1	**9**
Savignon	4	2	0	1	0	0	0	**7**
Spencer-Oatey	13	1	1	0	0	0	0	**15**
Ting-Toomey	9	2	2	0	0	0	1	**14**
Hofstede	5	0	0	0	0	0	0	**5**

8.3 Summary

This chapter focused on research questions 9a and 9b, which addressed aspects of MFL teachers' own educational background with regard to intercultural competence. The responses to question 9a, which asked if teachers had encountered IC during their own studies, revealed a nearly even split between the teachers who reported that they had encountered IC (44%) and those who had not (48%), with 8% selecting *don't know* and 1% preferring not to comment. Analysing the data from question 9a with regard to teachers' ages showed that of teachers aged under 40, more than 60% had encountered IC during their studies, while for those aged 40 or more, the opposite was the case, with more than 60% of them not having encountered IC during their studies. This ties in with the dates of publication of important books and articles on IC, such as Byram's 1997 monograph or Fantini's 1995 article, since there often is a delay between the publication of key texts and them being covered in seminars and lectures, as this may involve restructuring course components. On the other hand, the responses to question 9a do not suggest a link between coverage of IC in university education and the L2 taught, as the number of teachers who encountered IC or not tends to be nearly evenly split in most of the language groups.

The results of question 9b, which asked the MFL teachers to indicate whether they associated particular names with IC and also gave them the opportunity to add further names, showed that the clear majority of the teachers who responded (65%) associated Michael Byram with IC. Other scholars associated with IC that were selected or named by more than 10% of the teachers who responded were Helen Spencer-Oatey and Stella Ting-Toomey (both with 31%), Alvino Fantini and Sandra Savignon (both with 18%) and Geert Hofstede (12%). In addition, 23 other scholars were named, indicating that many of the teachers who answered this question were aware of a variety of researchers working in this field. The analysis of the findings based on the different language group showed that most of the more well-known scholars were known by teachers from at least three language groups, with Byram again being the most well-known scholar, since he was known by teachers in all language teacher groups (apart from the Dutch group, where no teachers responded to this question). Interestingly, Hofstede, whose name was noted by several teachers even though he was not included as a set option for selection in the survey, was only referred to by teachers of English.

References

Byram, M. (1997). *Teaching and assessing intercultural communicative competence*. Multilingual Matters.
Council of Europe. (2014). *Developing intercultural competence through education*. Council of Europe Publishing.
Fantini, A. E. (1995). Introduction—Language, culture and world view: Exploring the nexus. *International Journal of Intercultural Relations, 19*(2), 143–153.
Fantini, A. E. (2020). Language: An essential component of intercultural communicative competence. In J. Jackson (Ed.), *The Routledge handbook of language and intercultural communication* (2nd ed., pp. 267–278). Routledge.
Kelly, M. (2020). Intercultural second language teacher education. In J. Jackson (Ed.), *The Routledge handbook of language and intercultural education* (2nd ed., pp. 329–342). Routledge.
Moloney, R., Lobytsyna, M., & Moate, J. (2020). Looking for intercultural competences in language teacher education in Australia and Finland. In F. Dervin, R. Moloney, & A. Simpson (Eds.), *Intercultural competence in the work of teachers: Confronting ideologies and practices* (pp. 17–41). Routledge.
Savignon, S. J., & Sysoyev, P. V. (2005). Cultures and comparisons: Strategies for learners. *Foreign Language Annals, 38*(3), 357–365.
Sercu, L., Bandura, E., Castro, P., Davcheva, L., Laskaridou, C., Lundgren, U., García, M., & M. del C., & Ryan, P. (2005). *Foreign language teachers and intercultural competence: An international investigation*. Multilingual Matters.
UNESCO. (2013). *Intercultural competences: Conceptual and operational framework*. https://unesdoc.unesco.org/ark:/48223/pf0000219768

Open Access This chapter is licensed under the terms of the Creative Commons Attribution 4.0 International License (http://creativecommons.org/licenses/by/4.0/), which permits use, sharing, adaptation, distribution and reproduction in any medium or format, as long as you give appropriate credit to the original author(s) and the source, provide a link to the Creative Commons licence and indicate if changes were made.

The images or other third party material in this chapter are included in the chapter's Creative Commons licence, unless indicated otherwise in a credit line to the material. If material is not included in the chapter's Creative Commons licence and your intended use is not permitted by statutory regulation or exceeds the permitted use, you will need to obtain permission directly from the copyright holder.

CHAPTER 9

Conclusion

9.1 Summary of Findings

9.1.1 Chapter 4: Components of Intercultural Competence

Chapter 4 presented the results of questions 2 and 3 of the survey which focused on the general and linguistic components of IC. Question 2 contained 24 potential components of intercultural competence representing abilities, knowledge, skills and attitudes or characteristics that teachers could choose from. The results revealed that all items suggested as possible components of intercultural competence were selected by several teachers, thus indicating that all of them could feature in a IC framework. The most frequently chosen items were *awareness of different ways of thinking, orientations and values* (selected by 92% of the teachers), followed by *being understanding and sympathetic when encountering cultural differences* (87%) and *knowledge of politeness norms* (84%). In terms of links between IC and pragmatics, the item about politeness was selected third most often by participants, while *ability to produce situationally appropriate language* was in sixth place (out of 24), with 77% of the teachers considering it to be part of IC. This supports the notion of pragmatics as a key component of IC. The high scores awarded by the teachers in the individual language groups further strengthen this view.

Question 3 focused on the linguistic components of intercultural competence and included 12 items, of which five represented speech acts, two addressed aspects of impoliteness, two focused on emotions and three were likely to be treated as related to vocabulary. The results showed that the vast majority of the teachers considered the speech act items to be part of IC: conversational openings and closings (98%), apologies (97%), agreements and disagreements (92%), requests (89%) and complaints (86%). The two impoliteness-related items, *impolite and aggressive expressions* and *swear words and taboo language*, were each selected by 70% of the teachers, which again highlights the importance of including pragmatic components in intercultural competence models. This is again supported by the high number of teachers in the individual language groups who considered the pragmatics components to be part of IC.

9.1.2   Chapter 5: Aspects of L2 Teaching in Higher Education

Chapter 5 focused on questions 1, 4, 5 and 6 of the survey, all of which related to various aspects of teaching and had Likert-scale responses. Question 1 featured nine items, predominantly focused on academic skills but also addressing pragmatic and intercultural aspects, and asked teachers to assess the importance of these on a five-point Likert scale. The results revealed that the top three items that were rated as very important by the teachers were *general language skills* (58%), *academic writing skills* (55%) and *academic reading skills* (54%). In addition, these three items were also the only items that were rated as very important by more than half of the teachers. Combining those items that teachers had rated as very important or as important showed that two of the three top items considered to be very important were also among the top three in the combined ranking—namely, *academic reading skills* (90%) and *general language skills* (89%)—although their order was reversed. The new item in third place was *appropriate and sympathetic L2 expressions* (87%), highlighting the importance attached to pragmatics by the teachers. The results of the analysis according to the languages the teachers focused on revealed that, overall, the scores of the individual teacher groups did not tend to differ by more than one point from each other, nor did they differ much from the average score. However, it is important to keep in mind that the individual teacher groups differed considerably in size.

Question 6 asked the teachers to consider the importance of teaching a variety of language aspects and featured 19 items covering pragmatic as well as non-pragmatic aspects of language. The items considered to be very important by the most teachers were *situationally appropriate language*

(62%), followed by *everyday life vocabulary* (57%), with the two speech act items *conversational openings and closings* and *how to agree and disagree* in joint third place (51%). These items were also the only items that were rated to be very important by more than half of the teachers. The fact that three of the four items can be categorized as pragmatic further supports the notion that pragmatics is a key component of intercultural competence. Combining those items that teachers considered very important and important revealed that the top-ranked items largely remain the same, with the speech act of requests now joining the other speech acts in joint third place: *situationally appropriate language* (94%), *agreeing and disagreeing* (92%), followed by *everyday life vocabulary (90%)*, and two pragmatic items, *how to ask for something* and *conversational openings and closings* (both 89%). This further highlights teachers' beliefs in the significance of the pragmatic items for L2 teaching. The results of the language group analyses revealed that the scores of the individual groups did not tend to differ much.

Question 4 asked about the importance that MFL teachers assigned to teaching cultural facts about the places where the language in question is spoken as a native or official language. The question featured 16 items covering a variety of non-linguistic aspects. The results showed that there was only one item that was considered to be very important by more than half of the teachers, namely, *different ways of thinking, orientations and values* (60%). The next-most-frequent responses were supported by far fewer teachers: *literature, art and music* (27%) and *history* (20%). In addition, most of the teachers who did not rate *different ways of thinking, orientations and values* as very important rated it as important (with a combined rating of 94%). The analysis of the individual language group scores indicated broad agreement regarding the top-ranked item *different ways of thinking, orientations and values* across all languages. More interestingly, the language group scores indicated quite noticeable differences in the ratings of certain items (e.g., *biology and ecology; geography; literature, art and music*) based on the language taught by the participant.

Question 5, which asked about the importance of including different types of texts and materials in language classes, comprised 11 items covering a variety of topic areas. The three types of texts and materials considered to be very important by the highest number of teachers were *texts addressing study abroad experiences* (37%), *texts representing the views or experience of individuals with different ethnic backgrounds* (31%) and *equal representation of texts focusing on males and females* (30%). The combined importance scores also showed that the majority of the questionnaire items for this question were considered to be important or very important by more than half of the teachers. The analysis of the ratings by teachers who taught different languages revealed that the Spanish teachers considered all items to be either important or very important, while the Dutch and Swedish teachers had some of the lowest ratings, bearing in mind that these groups only contained three teachers each; there were relatively few major differences between the rating of different topic areas between teachers of languages that were represented by more than three teachers.

9.1.3   Chapter 6: The Relationship Between Intercultural and Pragmatic Competence

Chapter 6 presented the results of questions 7a and 7b, which explored MFL teachers' familiarity with pragmatics and how they perceived the connection—if any—between intercultural competence and pragmatic competence. The results of question 7a revealed that the majority of the teachers (68%) said that they were familiar with pragmatic competence, while 18% stated that they were not and 14% selected *don't know*. The analysis of MFL teachers' familiarity with pragmatic competence across the seven language groups showed that there were teachers in all groups that stated that they were familiar with the term. However, the percentage scores of the individual groups differed considerably, with 86% of the Spanish teachers indicating familiarity with the term but only 17% of the French teachers doing the same. However, group sizes need to be taken into consideration and larger-scale studies are needed to obtain more insights into teachers' conceptualizations of these terms across teachers of different L2s.

Question 7b included a definition of pragmatic competence and asked the teachers how—if at all—they believe that pragmatic competence and intercultural competence are linked. The clear majority of the teachers (86%) considered PC to be part of IC, 4 % considered IC to be part of PC and 2 % saw no link. The results of the language group analysis revealed that all teachers of four groups (German, French, Dutch and Swedish) considered pragmatic competence to be part of intercultural competence, while the clear majority of the remaining groups (English, Italian and Spanish) did likewise. The results of this chapter, therefore, show that the vast majority of the teachers see a link between intercultural and pragmatic competence.

9.1.4 Chapter 7: Intercultural Competence and Gender-Neutral Language

Chapter 7 presented the results of the survey questions 8a–8d, which focused on gender-neutral language. Question 8a examined whether MFL teachers believed that gender-neutral language options existed in the modern foreign languages that they taught. The results revealed that 64% of the teachers stated that these options existed in the language(s) they were teaching, while 25% said they did not, 6% chose *don't know* and 5% opted for the *other* option. The analysis of the seven language groups revealed that members of the individual language groups did not agree on whether gender-neutral language options existed in each specific L2, which was a surprising result.

Those participants who had answered that there were gender-neutral options were then asked about whether they taught these or not, and why. The responses showed that 73% of these teachers taught gender-neutral options, while 18% did not. Teachers teaching these options provided a variety of reasons, such as inclusion, equality, gender-neutral language being part of everyday language use, avoiding negative transfer from learners' L1, academic language conventions and it being part of the target language's culture, indicating that these teachers considered gender-neutral language to be linked to intercultural communicative competence and pragmatics.

A third of the teachers who did not teach gender-neutral language stated that they did not do so because they either talked about them in class but did not consider that to be teaching as such, or because gender-neutral options were covered in the materials anyway. Other teachers said that these options were not relevant in the respective language or would distract their learners. Only two teachers explicitly stated that they did not teach gender-neutral options because they disagreed with them; many others were interested in using them. Overall, the findings of the survey questions around gender-neutral language in Chap. 7 showed that this is an area worthy of further discussion in studies that address the interface between pragmatics and intercultural communicative competence.

9.1.5 Chapter 8: Intercultural Competence in Modern Foreign Language Teacher Education

Chapter 8 presented the results of research questions 9a and 9b that addressed whether intercultural competence was a relevant aspect of the

MFL teachers' own educational backgrounds. The responses to question 9a, which asked if teachers had encountered intercultural competence during their own university studies, showed a nearly even split between the teachers that had encountered it (44%) and those that had not (48%). To examine if the age of teachers played a role with regard to question 9a, I examined the data taking the teachers' ages into account. The results revealed that 60% of teachers aged under 40 had encountered IC during their studies, while 60% of teachers aged 40 or over had not. This suggests a link between coverage of IC in higher education programmes and the publications of key texts by Byram and Fantini in the late 1990s. However, there does not seem to be any link between the language that teachers taught and coverage of IC in their university education.

Question 9b, which asked teachers to indicate whether they associated particular names with IC, showed that the clear majority of the teachers (65%) associated Michael Byram with IC. Other scholars quite associated with IC were Helen Spencer-Oatey, Stella Ting-Toomey, Alvino Fantini, Sandra Savignon and Geert Hofstede. The participants also mentioned 23 other scholars, indicating that the teachers who responded to this question were aware of a range of researchers in this area. Most scholars were known by teachers who taught various different languages, with Byram once again being the most well-known scholar across language groups.

9.2 Limitations

In this section, I would like to address some limitations of the present study. One of the main limitations concerns the number of participants and the languages represented in the study. A higher number of participants teaching a wider variety of different modern foreign languages in different countries would have provided a fuller picture of the views of modern foreign language teachers in higher education. Some of the languages taught were only represented by a very small number of participants—in some cases even just a single teacher. A bigger sample size, with more educators teaching each individual language, would have enabled a contrastive analysis of a higher number of languages. In the present study, the seven MFLs that could sometimes be contrasted were all European languages of either Germanic or Romance origin. Thus, no group insights are available on MFL of other language families or from other parts of the world.

In addition, there are limitations around the survey. To begin with, it was only made available in English. As a consequence, only teachers that had a sufficient proficiency in English to understand and respond to the questions could take part in the study. The questionnaire also did not include an option for participants to leave their email address. While this decision was carefully taken, to ensure that anonymity could be guaranteed, it also meant that participants could not be contacted in order to clarify their answers or conduct a smaller-scale follow-up interview study based on their responses. In addition, certain questions were deliberately not included out of concerns that participants might feel that they could be identified if they provided that information. For example, questions were excluded that concerned the number and type of degrees the participants had and the years in which they completed their degree(s). However, this also meant that information on when participants completed their studies is only available indirectly by looking at the number of years they have been teaching, and the teachers' responses cannot be related to their level of education or type of degree.

9.3 Implications

9.3.1 Theoretical Implications

The results of the survey have shown that the clear majority of MFL teachers see a link between intercultural competence and pragmatics. Moreover, the majority of the teachers considered the pragmatics components included in questions 3 and 4 (analysed in Chap. 5) to be part of IC. That this view also impacted their opinions regarding the importance of teaching various components of pragmatics was shown in their responses to question 6 (discussed in Chap. 5). Key terms used in the definition of intercultural competence, such as "effective" and "appropriate" language use (Fantini, 1995, 2009), have always suggested a close relationship between pragmatic and intercultural competence, and the results of this study confirm that this view is in fact shared by the majority of teachers who participated here. Before suggesting a possible model of intercultural competence that features pragmatics, I would first like to present an overview in Fig. 9.1 of teachers' responses to the questions on components of intercultural competence that I suggested in questions 2 and 3, which provides information on the weighting of individual components—that is,

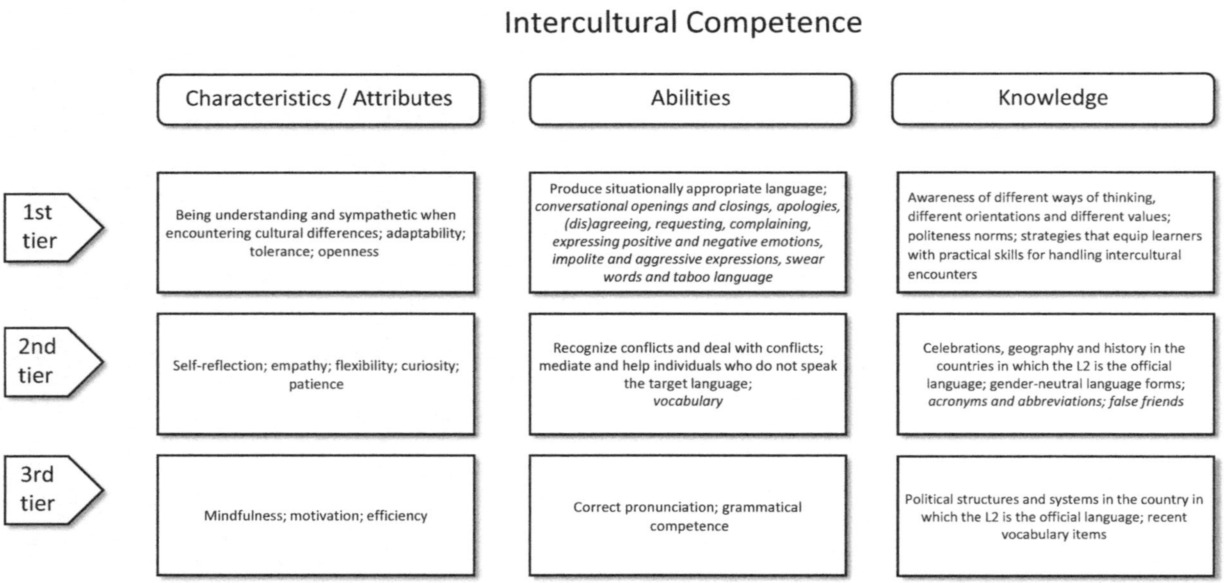

Intercultural Competence

	Characteristics / Attributes	Abilities	Knowledge
1st tier	Being understanding and sympathetic when encountering cultural differences; adaptability; tolerance; openness	Produce situationally appropriate language; conversational openings and closings, apologies, (dis)agreeing, requesting, complaining, expressing positive and negative emotions, impolite and aggressive expressions, swear words and taboo language	Awareness of different ways of thinking, different orientations and different values; politeness norms; strategies that equip learners with practical skills for handling intercultural encounters
2nd tier	Self-reflection; empathy; flexibility; curiosity; patience	Recognize conflicts and deal with conflicts; mediate and help individuals who do not speak the target language; vocabulary	Celebrations, geography and history in the countries in which the L2 is the official language; gender-neutral language forms; acronyms and abbreviations; false friends
3rd tier	Mindfulness; motivation; efficiency	Correct pronunciation; grammatical competence	Political structures and systems in the country in which the L2 is the official language; recent vocabulary items

Fig. 9.1 Three-tier model of intercultural competence (based on teachers' ratings)

which takes account of how many teachers considered each individual component to be part of IC.

The model includes all components listed in questions 2 and 3. The components featured in question 2 are presented in regular font, while the specific linguistic components addressed in question 3 are presented in italics. The components were categorized according to headings taken from Fantini's (2019) model. The three tiers represent the number of teachers who considered the individual components to be part of IC: first tier (more than 66%), second tier (more than 33%) and third tier (10–32%).

The model schematically illustrates that the majority of the components belonging to pragmatics are in the highest tier; for example, all the speech acts, as well as the impoliteness options. This again strengthens the case for considering pragmatics to be of key importance for IC and at the very core of it.

In addition, the model also provides insights on how teachers regard other components of intercultural competence frameworks (see Chap. 3 for details about the frameworks on which the questions were based). It shows that all of the components suggested were considered to be part of IC by at least 10% of the teachers.

Based on previous research on IC (see Chap. 2), and particularly influenced by the models of intercultural competence of Byram (1997, 2021) and Fantini (2019), as well as the results of the present study (including teachers' responses to questions that addressed their own teaching in Chap. 5 and their views on gender-neutral language in Chap. 7), I would like to propose a model of intercultural competence that places pragmatics in a prominent position next to established major categories, such as attributes/characteristics, skills, knowledge and linguistic competence. This model is presented in Fig. 9.2.

The model is in a circular form indicating that the interplay of the five components is essential for intercultural competence. I also agree with Fantini (2019), Deardorff (2006) and other researchers who consider the development of IC to be a continual process. My model subsumes all linguistic aspects other than pragmatics under the heading of "linguistic competence", and as such linguistic competence in my conceptualization does not solely refer to structural linguistic elements, such as grammar, but also includes sociolinguistic aspects and issues relevant to competence in specific areas, such as academic language skills. Gender-neutral language use is a potential hybrid between linguistic competence (in the sense that it refers to grammar and vocabulary) but also pragmatic competence (in

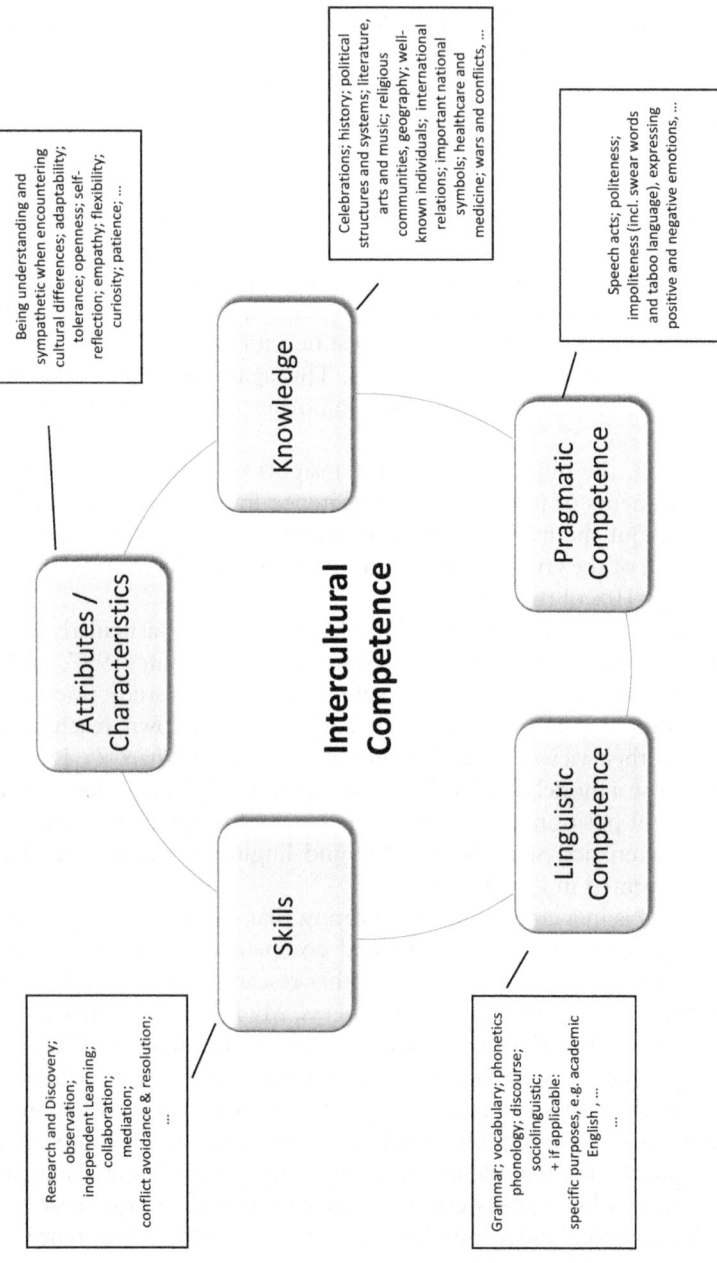

Fig. 9.2 Intercultural competence model

the sense that not using gender-neutral language can be perceived as offensive and inappropriate; as can using it, in some circumstances).

The skills, attributes and knowledge components mainly feature the subcomponents of questions 2 and 3, also presented in Fig. 9.1.[1] However, in the case of the knowledge components, I have also added in the cultural information components of question 5, as they represent aspects of L2 target country cultural information relevant for interactions with members of the target culture or sojourns in it.

Although my model of IC could be applied to various L2 teaching and learning contexts, it is based on the views of MFL teachers in higher education and therefore also intended to reflect issues particularly relevant to them, such as including components that are relevant for academic exchange programmes or study abroad sojourns.

9.3.2 Methodological Implications

As already mentioned in the limitations, the survey with which the data for this investigation were collected was only available in English. I had decided on an English-only survey after having conducted a study shortly before this one which used both an English and a German version of its questionnaire (Schauer, 2022). Since the aim of this study was to attract teachers teaching a wide variety of modern foreign languages, I was worried that having two language options might give the impression that I was primarily interested in English and German teachers, and therefore deter teachers of other modern foreign languages from taking part. It is difficult to evaluate in retrospect whether this concern was warranted or not. Future research on teachers representing different modern foreign languages may wish to consider translating questionnaires into a variety of different languages in order to make studies more accessible to teachers who do not feel comfortable and confident enough to take part in a study that requires a certain level of proficiency in English.

As also addressed in the limitations, the present study did not feature an option that would have allowed teachers to leave their contact details. Future studies may wish to include such an option, as it would make it possible to contact participants in case of queries or to conduct a

---

[1] See Chap. 2 and the methodology in Chap. 3 for more information on which frameworks inspired the questions in my survey, and thus also inspired the components and categories of the new IC model suggested here.

follow-up study. In order to ensure anonymity, questions that could potentially make it possible to find out who the individual teachers are were omitted in the present study (e.g., a specific question on the qualifications held by teachers). Future studies may wish to explore if more academic background information can be obtained while still ensuring anonymity for the participants.

9.3.3 Pedagogical Implications

The findings of the study have shown that the majority of MFL teachers working in higher education consider IC to be multifaceted and that they attach high importance to aspects of pragmatic competence. These are very encouraging results. However, the results have also revealed that (a) a number of teachers reported that they had not been exposed to intercultural competence during their studies—even in the lower age groups that would have entered higher education after the publication of seminal articles and books on the topic; (b) not all teachers were familiar with pragmatics; and (c) not all teachers were aware of developments regarding gender-neutral language in the language(s) that they taught.

In view of the position papers on intercultural competence by institutions such as UNESCO (2013) and the Council of Europe (2014), the prevalence of intercultural competence in MFL curricula and the wealth of research publications on the topic, higher educational institutions ought to ensure that they cover aspects of intercultural competence not only in their foreign language instruction programmes but also in their degree programmes that prepare students for future careers in the field of MFL teaching. In addition, individuals in managerial positions in such institutions ought to ensure that not only their teaching staff but also their administrative staff are familiar with intercultural competence and have skills and strategies at their disposal that will enable them to effectively and appropriately communicate with individuals who have other cultural and language backgrounds. This may mean that institutions have to invest in staff training programmes or self-study resources.

Appropriate and effective communication is not only at the heart of intercultural competence, it is also a key tenet in pragmatics. To ensure that teachers can prepare their students for intercultural communication, the teachers themselves need to have a solid foundation in pragmatics and at the very least need to be aware of how the most frequent speech acts are conventionally produced in the target language and what is considered to be polite or impolite in those countries in which the L2 is the official language that are particularly relevant for their students. This means that teachers need to encounter pragmatics during their own higher education studies.

Finally, I believe that teachers ought to keep themselves informed of important linguistic developments in the MFL they are teaching, especially if these developments could impact on their students' academic success or on how they are perceived. The use of gender-neutral language is one example for such a development in some of the MFLs covered in this study. Even if teachers themselves do not agree with gender-neutral language in modern foreign languages in which they constitute established and expected language use, such as English, they ought to ensure that from a certain proficiency level onwards, their students are aware of the relevant concepts and understand the basics (e.g., the use of *they* in English as a third person singular pronoun, in cases of unknown or non-binary gender identity). If students are not made aware of these developments, they may get confused about grammar rules, consider established academic writers to lack basic knowledge of grammar and form negative opinions of them, or receive negative feedback on their written work if the masculine form is used as a generic.

As Deardorff (2006) and Fantini (2019) have argued, intercultural competence is not something static but is a process. The same is true of language and culture—both develop and are subject to change. If we want our MFL learners to be able to communicate appropriately and effectively today and in the future, we need to make them aware that cultural norms, values and language use may change. How they react to these changes is up to them, but they ought to be able to make informed decisions about their language use and their conduct in the L2. And to be able to make an informed decision, they need precisely that—information. This is why the role of the MFL educator cannot be overestimated. By equipping their L2 learners with relevant skills, knowledge and information, they can help them become effective and appropriate intercultural communicators and can open up a vast array of opportunities.

References

Byram, M. (1997). *Teaching and assessing intercultural communicative competence*. Multilingual Matters.

Byram, M. (2021). *Teaching and assessing intercultural communicative competence revisited* (2nd ed.). Multilingual Matters.

Council of Europe. (2014). *Developing intercultural competence through education*. Council of Europe Publishing.

Deardorff, D. K. (2006). Identification and assessment of intercultural competence as a student outcome of internationalization. *Journal of Studies in International Education*, *10*(3), 241–266. https://doi.org/10.1177/1028315306287002

Fantini, A. E. (1995). Introduction—Language, culture and world view: Exploring the nexus. *International Journal of Intercultural Relations*, *19*(2), 143–153.

Fantini, A. E. (2009). Assessing intercultural competence: Issues and tools. In D. K. Deardorff (Ed.), *The SAGE handbook of intercultural competence* (pp. 456–476). Sage.

Fantini, A. E. (2019). *Intercultural communicative competence in educational exchange: A multinational perspective*. Routledge.

Schauer, G. A. (2022). Intercultural competence and pragmatics in the L2classroom: Views of in-service EFL teachers in primary, secondary and adult education. In T. McConachy & A. J. Liddicoat (Eds.), *Teaching and learning second language pragmatics for intercultural understanding* (pp. 173–191). Routledge.

UNESCO. (2013). *Intercultural competence: Conceptional and operational framework*. https://unesdoc.unesco.org/ark:/48223/pf0000219768

Open Access This chapter is licensed under the terms of the Creative Commons Attribution 4.0 International License (http://creativecommons.org/licenses/by/4.0/), which permits use, sharing, adaptation, distribution and reproduction in any medium or format, as long as you give appropriate credit to the original author(s) and the source, provide a link to the Creative Commons licence and indicate if changes were made.

The images or other third party material in this chapter are included in the chapter's Creative Commons licence, unless indicated otherwise in a credit line to the material. If material is not included in the chapter's Creative Commons licence and your intended use is not permitted by statutory regulation or exceeds the permitted use, you will need to obtain permission directly from the copyright holder.

Index[1]

A
Abrams, Z., 15
Academic language skills, 71, 143
Academic reading skills, 72, 74, 90, 136
Academic vocabulary, 75, 79
Academic writing skills, 46, 72, 74, 90, 136
Achiba, M., 11
Acronyms and abbreviations, 47, 48, 62, 64, 75, 79
Adaptability, 46, 57, 60
Address terms, 14, 17, 18, 18n10
Age, 11, 16, 39, 43, 48, 51, 85, 86, 89, 92, 126–128, 146
Agreeing and disagreeing, 62, 63, 67, 75, 76, 91, 136, 137
Apologies, 10, 13, 62, 63, 67, 75, 79, 136
Appropriate, 1, 8–10, 14, 18n10, 19n11, 20n12, 27, 29, 46, 48, 49, 56, 57, 60, 61, 67, 71, 72, 74–76, 78, 79, 90, 91, 109, 112, 113, 117, 118, 135, 136, 141, 146, 147
Appropriateness, 21, 22, 27, 28
Artistic products, 15, 16, 82
Attitudes, 8, 9, 15, 16, 24, 61, 66, 135
Attributes, 143
Austin, J.L., 13

B
Bachman, L.F., 20, 21
Bardovi-Harlig, K., 7, 10, 13, 14, 62n2, 96
Barron, A., 7, 11, 17
Behavioural taboos, 16
Being understanding and sympathetic when encountering cultural differences, 46, 54, 57, 60, 66, 135
Beliefs, 8, 9, 15, 16, 48

---

[1] Note: Page numbers followed by 'n' refer to notes.

© The Author(s) 2024
G. A. Schauer, *Intercultural Competence and Pragmatics*,
https://doi.org/10.1007/978-3-031-44472-2

Bias, 105, 108, 118, 119
Biology and ecology, 47, 80, 83, 91–92, 137
Blum-Kulka, S., 9, 95
Byram, M., 22–30, 23n16, 25n17, 27n19, 47n6, 49, 53, 57, 64, 80, 81, 125, 129–132, 140, 143

C
Canale, M., 20, 20n12, 21
CCSARP, 9, 13
Celce-Murcia, M., 8
Celebrations, 46, 47, 56, 58, 81, 84
Clyne, M., 12
Cohen, A.D., 11n5, 13, 14, 95
Communicative competence, 19–21, 21n13, 23, 29, 30
Communicative language teaching, 19, 19n11
Complaining, 62, 65, 75, 79
Complaints, 62, 63, 67, 76, 136
Conflicts, 46, 56, 57, 67
Contexts, 8–10, 11n4, 12–14, 17, 20n12, 21, 27, 41, 42, 46, 48, 145
Council of Europe, 1, 17, 53, 80, 81, 85, 146
Cross-cultural pragmatics, 9, 10
Crozet, C., 65n3
Crystal, D., 9, 9n2
Culpeper, J., 7, 10
Cultural differences, 71, 72
Culturally appropriate language, 118
Culture, 13–19, 24, 26, 29, 48, 80, 82, 85, 85n1, 86, 88, 112, 113, 116, 118, 139, 145, 147
Culture shock, 85, 86
Curiosity, 46, 56, 57
Curricula, 30, 53, 101, 146

D
Deardorff, D.K., 4n3, 22, 30, 30n20, 53, 57, 143, 147
Dewaele, J.M., 19, 62
Different ways of thinking, orientations and values, 46, 54, 56, 59, 66, 80, 81, 91, 135, 137
Disabilities, 48, 86, 89
Diversity, 17, 23, 58, 60, 80, 85, 85n1, 102, 113
Diversity competence, 23, 80
Dorjee, T., 47n6, 53
Dutch, 2, 39, 44, 57, 59–61, 64–67, 78, 79, 83, 84, 88, 89, 92, 96, 100, 102, 107, 108, 111, 128, 129, 131, 132, 138

E
Economidou-Kogetsidis, M., 61, 95
Education, 1–3, 12n6, 19, 20, 23, 29, 42, 44, 45, 51, 54, 58, 64, 67, 71, 73, 78, 91, 97, 101, 125–129, 131, 132, 136–138, 140, 141, 145–147
Effective, 8–10, 27, 29, 49, 141, 146, 147
Efficiency, 46, 54
Emotions, 8, 9, 18, 47, 48, 62, 64, 66, 67, 78, 80, 136
Empathy, 46, 56, 57
English, 2, 10–13, 12n6, 12n7, 17–20, 18n9, 26, 27, 39, 42, 44–46, 50, 54, 56–61, 64–67, 78, 79, 83, 84, 89, 96, 97, 97n1, 100, 102, 105, 107–109, 111, 112, 114, 116–119, 121, 128, 129, 131, 132, 138, 141, 145, 147
Equality, 113, 116–118, 120, 139
Ethnic backgrounds, 86, 89, 92, 137
Ethnicity, 11, 16, 85
European Parliament, 105n1

F

False friends, 62, 64–66, 75, 79
Fantini, A.E., 22, 23n16, 27–30, 47n6, 49, 53, 57, 64, 125, 129, 130, 132, 140, 141, 143, 147
Félix-Brasdefer, J.C., 8, 9, 11, 13n8, 29, 64, 97
Flexibility, 46, 56, 57
Franklin, P., 15
French, 2, 10, 12, 26, 39, 44, 50, 51, 57, 59–61, 64, 65, 67, 78, 79, 84, 89, 90, 96, 97, 97n1, 100–102, 107, 111, 113, 117, 119, 120, 128, 129, 131, 138

G

Gender, 11, 16, 39, 46, 49, 56, 60, 85, 88, 105, 105n1, 107, 110, 111, 113–121, 139
Gender fair language, 105n1, 108
Gender inclusive language, 105n1, 106
Gender-neutral, 56, 106–108, 110–112, 114–121, 139
Gender-neutral language, 3, 17, 46, 49, 56, 57, 60, 67, 105–121, 105n1, 139, 143, 145–147
General language skills, 46, 71, 72, 74, 90, 136
Generic, 105, 107, 109
Geography, 46, 47, 56, 58, 83, 92, 137
German, 2, 10–12, 12n6, 12n7, 17, 18, 18n9, 18n10, 20, 39, 44, 46, 48, 50, 56, 57, 59, 60, 64, 65, 78, 79, 83, 84, 89, 96, 97, 97n1, 100, 102, 106–109, 111, 112, 114, 117, 119–121, 128, 129, 131, 138, 145
Germany, 112, 120
Glaser, K., 11, 95

Grammar, 48, 56, 58, 75, 78, 79, 112, 113, 117, 119, 120, 143, 147
Grammatical competence, 20, 21
Greetings, 12–14, 16, 18n9, 62, 65

H

History, 15, 16, 46, 47, 56, 58, 80, 91, 137
Houck, N.R., 13
House, J., 9, 18, 64, 95, 97
Hughes, R., 17

I

IC, 1, 24, 26, 28–30, 53, 57, 58, 61, 63, 64, 66, 67, 98, 100, 101, 127, 129, 130, 132, 135, 146
ICC, 26, 30, 125
Identity, 17, 39, 113, 118, 120
Immigrants, 48, 86, 88, 89, 92
Impolite, 18–20, 47, 48, 136, 146
Impolite and aggressive expressions, 75, 76, 79
Impoliteness, 18, 62, 64, 67
Inappropriate, 13, 18, 20
Inappropriateness, 18
Inclusion, 112, 113, 116, 120, 139
Inclusive, 105n1, 109, 112, 113, 117, 119, 120
Intentions, 8, 9
Intercultural, 72, 80, 90
Intercultural communication, 146
Intercultural communicative competence, 22–27, 22n15, 116, 125, 128, 139
Intercultural competence, 1–3, 4n3, 8, 14, 20, 22–25, 22n15, 27, 29, 46, 47, 47n6, 49, 53–66, 74, 77, 78, 80, 81, 85, 91, 92, 95, 98–102, 113, 120, 125–132, 135, 137, 138, 140, 141, 143, 146, 147

Intercultural encounters, 56, 58, 72, 74
Interlanguage, 10
Interlanguage pragmatics, 9–11, 11n5, 13, 20
Ishihara, N., 11n5, 13, 14
Italian, 2, 39, 44, 50, 57, 59, 60, 64–67, 78, 79, 83, 84, 89, 96, 97, 100, 102, 107, 111, 113, 114, 117, 120, 121, 128, 129, 131, 138

J
Jackson, J., 1, 22, 23, 27, 61, 98

K
Kádár, D., 9
Kasper, G., 9, 95

L
Lee, C., 11
Legal system, 47, 83
LGBTIQ, 48, 86, 88–90
LGBTIQA, 113
Liddicoat, A.J., 1, 16–18, 22n14, 23n16, 47n6, 53, 61, 65n3, 80, 85, 98
Linguistic competence, 25, 64, 66, 143
Literature, 15, 21n13, 82
Literature, art and music, 47, 80, 82, 83, 91, 137
L2, 53–62, 65, 72, 74, 80, 81
L2 pragmatics, 9–11

M
Martínez Flor, A., 13, 95
McConachy, T., 1, 22n14, 23n16, 45, 61, 98

Mindfulness, 46, 56, 60
Morollón Martí, N., 18, 64
Morphology, 20, 21
Motivation, 46, 56
Mugford, G., 18, 64
Myrset, A., 11

N
National symbols, 47, 81, 83, 84
Negative emotions, 62, 65, 75, 79
Negative transfer, 113, 116, 139
Non-sexist language, 105n1
Norms, 12, 14, 16, 18n9, 19, 20n12, 21, 54, 56, 57, 59, 60, 64, 66, 67, 135, 147
Norwegian, 41, 120

O
Offensive language, 18, 145
Olshtain, E., 8, 95
Openings and closings, 47, 48, 62, 63, 67, 75, 76, 79, 91, 136, 137
Openness, 46, 54, 56, 57, 60

P
Palmer, A.S., 20, 21
Patience, 46, 56, 57, 60
Paulston, C.B., 13n8, 20
Perceptions, 10, 15, 18, 19
Phonology, 20
Piepho, H.E., 20
Polite, 1, 146
Politeness, 8, 9, 22, 46, 54, 56, 57, 59–61, 66, 67, 74, 135, 136
Political structures and systems, 46, 47, 56, 58
Positive emotions, 62, 65, 75, 79
Pragmatic, 1–3, 74, 76, 78, 90, 113, 120, 136

Pragmatic competence, 1, 3, 14, 21, 27, 29, 44, 48, 49, 60, 66, 67, 76, 78, 80, 92, 95–101, 138
Pragmatics, 1–3, 7–10, 13, 19n11, 20, 20n12, 21, 23, 27–29, 27n19, 53, 61–63, 66, 67, 71, 74, 76, 80, 90, 91, 95, 97, 113, 114n6, 116, 136–139, 141, 143, 146
Pronoun, 107, 112, 119, 121
Pronunciation, 46, 56, 58, 75, 78, 79

R
Regions, 11, 12, 48
Religion, 16, 85
Religious beliefs, 86, 88, 89
Requests, 10, 11, 13, 62, 63, 67, 75, 136, 137
Roever, C., 1, 9, 10, 13, 98
Romance languages, 59, 108, 120
Rose, K.R., 11

S
Savić, M., 11
Savignon, S.J., 20, 49, 125, 129, 130, 132, 140
Savoirs, 26
Savvidou, C., 61, 95
Scarino, A., 16–18, 47n6, 53, 80, 85
Schauer, G.A., 7, 10, 11, 18, 18n10, 22, 23, 27, 27n19, 45, 47n6, 54, 61, 67, 109, 114n6, 145
Schneider, K.P., 11
Second language pragmatics, 9, 11
Self-reflection, 46, 56, 57, 60
Semantics, 8, 20
Sercu, L., 15, 16, 50n7, 80, 82, 127n1
Sexuality, 16, 85
Shively, R., 8, 9

Skills, 10, 66, 71, 72, 74, 135, 136, 143, 145–147
Sociolinguistic, 20, 21, 24, 25, 143
Sociolinguistic competence, 21
Spanish, 2, 10–12, 12n6, 39, 44, 50, 57, 59–61, 64, 65, 67, 78, 79, 84, 88, 89, 92, 96, 97, 100–102, 106, 107, 111, 113, 120, 128, 129, 131, 138
Speech act theory, 13
Speech acts, 13, 14, 61, 62, 64, 66, 67, 76, 78, 91, 135, 137, 143, 146
Spencer-Oatey, H., 15, 23, 27, 49, 65n3, 98, 129, 130, 132, 140
Strategies that equip learners with practical skills for handling intercultural encounters, 46, 58, 71
Study abroad, 48, 85, 86, 88, 89, 92, 145
Swain, M., 20, 20n12, 21
Swear words, 19, 47, 48, 62, 64, 67, 75, 77, 79, 136
Swedish, 2, 18n9, 20, 39, 44, 57, 59–61, 64–67, 78, 79, 83, 84, 88, 89, 92, 96, 100, 102, 106–109, 111, 113, 120, 121, 128, 129, 131, 138
Syntax, 8, 20, 21, 48

T
Taboo language, 19, 47, 48, 62, 64, 65, 67, 75–77, 79, 136
Taguchi, N., 1, 9, 29, 98
Target language proficiency, 30, 64
Tatsuki, D.H., 13
Teacher education, 129, 146
Teacher training, 125, 128
Ting-Toomey, S., 47n6, 49, 53, 129, 130, 132, 140

Tolerance, 46, 56, 57
Trosborg, A., 15

U
UNESCO, 1, 53, 125, 146
Usó Juan, E., 13, 95

V
Values, 9, 15, 16, 24, 47, 112, 113, 116, 118, 137, 147

Variational pragmatics, 9, 11, 12, 14
Vocabulary, 21, 46–48, 56, 58, 60, 62, 64, 65, 67, 75, 76, 78, 79, 88, 91, 112, 118, 136, 137, 143

W
Warga, M., 11, 97n1
Wars and conflicts, 47, 80, 83

SPRINGER NATURE

GPSR Compliance

The European Union's (EU) General Product Safety Regulation (GPSR) is a set of rules that requires consumer products to be safe and our obligations to ensure this.

If you have any concerns about our products, you can contact us on ProductSafety@springernature.com

In case Publisher is established outside the EU, the EU authorized representative is:

Springer Nature Customer Service Center GmbH
Europaplatz 3
69115 Heidelberg, Germany

The manufacturer's authorised representative in the EU is Springer Nature Customer Service Centre GmbH, Europaplatz 3, 69115 Heidelberg, Germany. If you have any concerns regarding our products, please contact ProductSafety@springernature.com

Printed and bound by CPI Group (UK) Ltd, Croydon, CR0 4YY
23/03/2026
02076355-0012